HERE AND NOW

An Approach to Christian Healing through Gestalt

IAN DAVIDSON

Foreword by Richard Holloway

DARTON, LONGMAN AND TODD
LONDON

First published in 1991 by
Darton, Longman and Todd Ltd
89 Lillie Road, London SW6 1UD

British Library Cataloguing in Publication Data
Davidson, Ian
  Here and now : an approach to Christian Healing through
  Gestalt.
  1. Spiritual healing
  I. Title
  615.852

  ISBN 0–232–51929–3

Phototypeset by
Input Typesetting Ltd, London SW19 8DR
Printed and bound in Great Britain by
Courier International Ltd, Tiptree, Essex

Almighty God,
whose Son revealed in signs and miracles
the wonder of your saving love:
renew your people with your heavenly grace,
and in all our weakness,
sustain us by your mighty power;
through Jesus Christ our Lord.
(Collect for Epiphany 3 ASB)

CONTENTS

FOREWORD

The best teachers all have a capacity for revelation, for uncovering what is hidden or illuminating what is obscure. They show us what we already know, but have not acknowledged or fully comprehended. The parables of Scripture have this same capacity: they illuminate our condition and challenge our illusions. 'Thou art the man', said Nathan to King David. 'Go and do thou likewise', said Jesus to all of us.

Ian Davidson has written a revelatory book. And it is revelatory in two senses. It lets us in on the mysteries of psychotherapy, especially on the apparently mystifying Gestalt method. Read this book and you will actually feel how it works. But it does more than that. It actually helps to illuminate our own condition. We are all wounded and this book will help us to understand why; and it will encourage us to seek wholeness.

But the most important thing about this book is that it does not leave us on our own, no matter how tried and tested our therapies are. It is a book about Grace, which is the name Christians give to God's action in their lives, co-operating with the human will to be whole. Ian Davidson has written a profound and helpful book. I commend it warmly.

Richard Holloway
Bishop of Edinburgh

ACKNOWLEDGEMENTS

To all who have helped and encouraged me in the production of this book;

To Gill, my wife, for her support and patience whilst living with 'Christian Gestalt';

To all who took the risk of launching 'Christian Growth and Gestalt' conferences by leading groups – or assisting . . . John, Chris, Di, Ruth, Marie, Sharon, Tom, Pat, Felicity, Angela, David, Jan, Mike, Miles, Sheila and Sue;

To those who allowed their work scripts to be used – they will recognise themselves but remain anonymous;

To Nick Isbister for supervision, suggestions, scrutiny; and John Richards for encouragement and proof-reading;

To the Council and Community of Scargill House for giving me time to write;

To Janet Wordsworth, Gill Driver and Patricia Richardson for their skill with manuscripts and word processors.

Thank you

INTRODUCTION

THIS BOOK CAME TO BE written as a result of fifteen years spadework in the prayer counselling and inner-healing movement within the current Renewal across the Church of God. I am specially indebted to Frank Lake and Anne White for early teaching and to my colleagues in later years, John Bedford and Chris Andrew, who have pioneered with me the kind of events described in this book, firstly, at Bedford and latterly, at Scargill House in Yorkshire.

The book is written for counsellors and those who are training to be counsellors. It will also be of help to ministers and those with responsibilities for pastoral care. To the lay person interested in health and wholeness I would say, 'Pick and choose . . . feel free to skip the learning boxes – but don't miss Chapter 12!' The first and most important lesson which people-helpers learn is their *own* need for healing and growth. A group-experience which includes this therapy is a vital part of a complete training experience. We learn by the experience of being in a group, taking part in workshops. A book is no substitute.

Jesus called individuals into *a group* and this became the context which would change their lives. Within this group each disciple was dealt with in a very personal way according to his need and personality. Jesus spoke in colourful, earthy ways, told stories, challenged people to think again and helped them to manage a process of change and often painful growth. In each chapter here I offer someone's real life situation. The dialogue part is followed by my own comments and an evaluation of what took place, together with a teaching-summary for counsellors. It may help the reader unfamiliar with 'groups' to begin the book by reading Chapter 1 and then Chapter 10. May the encounters recorded here open doors to the reader's own lively and life-changing encounters yet to come.

The Scripture verses are to highlight what has happened, or to act as a mirror-reflection. God's Word is always a commentary and a companion in life, and sometimes a challenge pointing the way further ahead.

The section headed 'Bringing it Home' is for personal use. The questions may prove useful for self-examination and reflection, or even as a basis for weekly group study and discussion. *On its own*, however, the book does not equip anyone for group therapy, or for ministry to individuals. Each chapter ends with a prayer.

The group I gather in Chapter 2 is composed of real people – the dialogues are genuine, but all names have been changed. It is the group which gives authority to the leader to work, allowing him or her to come alongside or to go ahead. Such a privilege depends always on the trust of the group and the permission each person gives for its leader to take authority physically, emotionally and spiritually.

I do not avoid earthy language and four-letter words on one hand nor 'God-talk' and an emphasis on prayer, on the other. I believe, in God's economy, earth and heaven are bound together. Our route to the heavenly city starts right where we are with our feet firmly on the ground. But even here we have glimpses and foretastes of the road ahead. We need to 'tell it like it is' in both directions.

There remains a question . . . 'Does it all last – is the work recounted in this book of permanent value in the lives of those who do it?' Imagery and guided meditation may be very powerful in situ, but what happens when I get back to daily life?

A friend writes as follows: 'Each experience of God is like a camera shutter opening, then closing again. As our faith gets stronger so the shutter stays open longer, but that does not affect the reality of what the shutter reveals.' I like to think of many of the experiences described in this book as colour photographs which can be kept and carried in one's handbag or wallet for constant reference. '*This happened to me*, I have a permanent image of it in front of me, it will affect my understanding of who I am and the new freedom in which I can live.' Some of us are lucky enough to live frequently in a state of what Ruth Burrows calls 'light on' in relationship to God, but most of us are more familiar with the experience she calls 'light off'. However, we have seen the light and can remember it well enough to be guided by it and led on to the next time of disclosure.

You will read a vignette of a life in each chapter – not in historical detail, but in all the immediate exposure that an X-Ray camera gives. 'Broken bones', 'strained ligaments' or 'missing parts' are obvious. They become obvious by dialogue in which the group and its facilitator use all their faculties of attentiveness, response and loving confrontation. The broken heart, the resignation or despair, the frustration or seething anger within are revealed. Be prepared for something other than polite conversation! The dialogue is workmanlike, pointed, sometimes abrupt. It is often dramatic, seldom boring. The steps through which it carries the participant – from a first tentative exploration of a 'problem' to a triumphant 'I see it all now', are outlined in Chapter 1.

Look out for the 'healing steps' in each dialogue that follows, and for the sense of completion or 'job-done' at the end of each episode. A glimpse of personal truth, or a special revelation has been shared. It is for the receiver to value it and to assimilate it into life. May the stories and questions encourage you to find that 'Approach to Christian Healing' which lies ahead for yourself, and those you desire to help.

Chapter One

WHAT IS INNER HEALING? – AND GESTALT?

MOST OF US like to be regarded as people helpers. You are probably reading this book because you want to learn all you can about ways to do it, or to do it more effectively. If, like me, you flip through a book backwards you may have started at the heavy end first. Take heart, begin at the beginning and go through at your own pace, meeting the people in turn. You will find them interesting, frustrating, lovable and often so understandable. 'It's like me, I do that, I feel just like that sometimes.' You will meet them each in their human predicament and identify frequently. You may be encouraged at the way they come through. As Ministers, counsellors and health professionals we can all improve our helping skills so look out for new insights on how it's done.

Whatever your remit in life, this book encourages the concept of 'The Wounded Healer'. To qualify I need to know how hurt *I* am, where I can get help, and how to pass this on to others. Such learning, like any good advice, is best received by the teaspoonful rather than the bucketful. It is also best received through a personal story. I want these stories to speak for themselves and to keep my comments to a minimum. The Bible's most dramatic sequences are memorable for their dialogues. The story of Nathan confronting King David (2 Sam. 12) and the simple vivid conversation piece we call the 'Prodigal Son' (Luke 15:11) both use the spoken word to make their indelible impression, 'You are the man!' 'Quick, bring the best robe!' There is nevertheless a grounding of theory and assumption which needs to be spelt out before I introduce you to Tim, Jane and the rest of the group, with their extended dialogues.

Let us first picture the human personality as a house. For our purpose the house has three levels: there is a cellar, a living-room and an attic. In the cellar I keep all my childhood memories and impressions. Down there I find the freedom and joy I felt in childhood, but also I can encounter rage, panic, lust, dread, hunger and all manner of anxieties.

The floor of my living-room is well boarded over, but there is a trapdoor and steps lead down to the cellar. All the hidden aspects of childhood are there in each one of us and it is a simple matter, once we have discovered the trapdoor, to encounter them, to encourage them to come up for the light, fresh air and loving care they may need in the living-room. For shorthand we call this area 'the feeling child'.

The living-room is the *adult* part of my mind. Here I think, choose and decide in a rational manner. Here I can process the information coming to me from the world outside. Here I can decide how to handle the emotions coming up from below as soon as I have become aware of them. In this the adult and 'computing' part of my personality I can also hear the Holy Spirit's voice. When I first become a Christian it is within this part of myself that I learn to dialogue with the Lord.

Above the living-room, in the attic, live my 'parents'. In this part of my personality live all the rules and regulations I have ever heard and felt obliged to comply with or rebel against. Mother's voice, and father's, echo in turn from this place. Sometimes they quarrel. All I have ever perceived of God's law, human law and my own personal requirements of myself, my own standards, are here in serried ranks of dos and don'ts, shoulds, oughts, musts and 'got-tos'. This part of my make-up warns me of dangers, tells me when to stop, gives me limits and boundaries. More positively, from here come nurturing and encouraging noises which will often prompt me to do better than I thought I could.

To live comfortably in my 'house' I need access to all three areas and I need an equilibrium and balance. The parents' voices need to be attended to, the child's feelings need to be

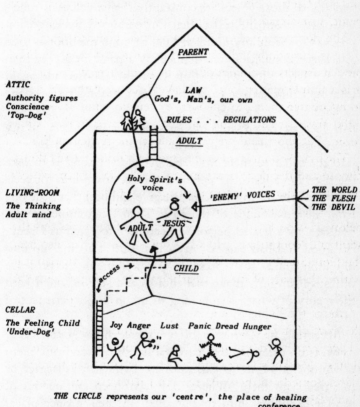

THE HOUSE WE LIVE IN: THE VOICES WITHIN

THE CIRCLE represents our 'centre', the place of healing
conference.
BRING DOWN the 'parents' to talk to.
BRING UP the 'child' to talk to.
LISTEN to the Holy Spirit, the words of Jesus.
TUNE-OUT enemy voices.

expressed and their energy used profitably. In my living-room there needs to be space for adult conversations and dialogues with my spiritual self. When any part of me becomes over-dominant or neglected I am in trouble. If, for example, my attic voices dominate my whole house with *rules*, the feeling child is shut out and my life feels colourless and dull. If those voices are constantly challenged by a 'rebellious brat' from the cellar then I'm paralysed by indecision – I can't make up my mind. If I fall through the floor-boards and become totally overwhelmed by a panic or a rage then I'm not safe to live with – I'm near to breakdown and again lose my adult power to choose. Inner healing restores the balance.

If I accept the presence of Christ, healer and helper, in my 'living-room', then I can invite him to come step by step into the cellar to meet my feeling child. Healing is to take the risen Lord Jesus, by personal choice, down into the feeling child area, to love, accept, forgive and heal that little one from all the wounds of the past. Then I can come up and live free, as a healed person. I become integrated as I bring the good and bad parts of my child, one at a time, up into my adult mind, not repressing or rejecting. In the presence of Jesus I can now make real choices and stay in touch with the reality of what is happening to me in my experiences of life.

Accepting his Lordship of the whole house I can bring down from the attic those parental 'voices'. I can bring them down one at a time to talk to them. I choose to disagree or to agree with them. Where they have been getting out of hand I can allow him to put them in their proper place. Where I have been ignoring them I hear him reinforcing proper demands.

So I come together and become whole. But if I let go the control of my mind and, as it were, fall down through rotten floor-boards into my cellar, I can get lost in random feelings and the many lost childhood aspects of my past. I lose touch with my adult self and also with the presence of other people and Jesus. I can become a disintegrated and separated person. I will feel alone and helpless, I will be suffering *breakdown* instead of constructive and healing breakthrough. In a similar way, if I simply allow my parent voices to run me around and condition me to distrust any feelings I might have from below, I can so easily become a robot, moving through life without any real joy or compassion, without any capacity for feeling myself, or acknowledging and understanding the feelings of others. I may know all the right answers and keep all the rules punctiliously, but inside I feel dry and lost, like an owl in the desert. In this case people have ruled out part of their nature, and may well spend much of their lives seeking a counterfeit or substitute. Many of the addictions, ranging from alcohol to overwork, are chosen in this way.

Inner healing brings parent and child voices into a harmonious family conference within me, with Jesus as leader, teacher, healer and Lord.

In a nutshell definition emotional healing is bringing the Jesus of now into the experiences of the *past* (which still overflow and control *present* responses and condition), in such a way that our guilt is forgiven, our bondages are broken, our captivity is turned into deliverance and our brokenness is turned into wholeness by the revelation and anointing of the Lord to our hearts so that we can walk in newness of life. Newness of life dawns gradually, like the coming of a new day. The phrase, 'it began to dawn on me that . . .', is far more common on an inner healing journey than, 'suddenly I was changed'. Healings *can* take place suddenly with a 'whoosh', but far more often they are the product of gradual step by step realisations within a person, as he or she walks forward, shaking off old fears, wrong beliefs, negative emotions and discovering in a very personal way the possibilities of freedom, love and hope.

'Do I need inner healing?' some may ask at this point. 'Does *everyone* need it? – Surely we are saved by God's grace and by our faith in the finished work of Christ?' Insofar as our parenting was 'good enough' and our faith is adequate; insofar as we are getting by in life without major hiccoughs, then perhaps the answer is 'No'. But, if you perceive your salvation as a process over time, and heed Paul's admonition to 'work at it' (Phil. 2:12–13) and to 'press on' (Phil. 3:12–14)

– then you will be keen to explore all the blessings, healings, and deliverances implicit in accepting Christ as your Saviour. Each personality working in this book is already committed. Each would say at the end of his or her session, 'Praise God, now I have experienced more of what I already believe!'

Many of the techniques and procedures illustrated in this book have a secular origin. Sometimes my therapist friends say, 'Why bring God into it at all?' Perhaps they see the religious words and God-talk as some kind of boundary or limitation. In my experience and working mainly with church-going people, the dimension we call God, the spiritual power we call Holy, and the risen, healing life we call 'Jesus' is my main source of effectiveness. In saying this I am only too well aware that sometimes prayer can be an escape and religious language mere rhetoric, but so can any other language – psychiatric, scientific or medical. It is up to us to discern when real communication is taking place and when it is not. 'Why bring God into all this?' seems an unnecessary question. He is already here – and usually ahead of us! I consider in depth the ways and the words of Jesus to confirm this assertion in Chapter 12.

The great psychologist Carl Jung once declared that he knew no one in the second half of his life whose predicament was not ultimately helped or healed by achieving a religious outlook on life.

The beginning of the process is always the simple unspec-tacular art of listening, – what Henri Nouwen has called 'the highest form of hospitality'. In *Life Together*, Bonhoeffer wrote,

> The first service that one owes to others in the fellow-ship consists in listening to them. Just as love for God begins with listening to his Word, so the beginning of love for the brethren is learning to listen to them. It is God's love for us that he not only gives us his Word, but he also lends us his ear. Christians, especially ministers . . . often forget that listening can be a greater service than speaking.

'When a plaintiff brings to you his case do not dismiss him

until he has swept out his body. A good hearing is a soothing of the heart.' It sounds biblical, but was in fact some advice given by his Grand Vizier to the King of Egypt in the year 2450 BC. This is the way all inner healing begins – a careful, attentive listening, a patience of spirit willing not to judge, not to interrupt and never to appear shocked or condemning at what one might hear. All of us, amateur or professional helpers alike, need constantly to review our listening skills and to be improving our quality of empathy* and genuineness. As we listen we discern a pattern in what is spoken. There appear to be salient features about this person's reaction to life which recur time and time again. It is as if certain themes, certain family mottos, like the instructions coded into DNA molecules, run through a person's life, producing the same consequences again and again. If you chop a slice from a cucumber around the middle you will find a pattern of pips. You may slice the cucumber anywhere from one end to the other and the pattern will be the same. Or, to change the analogy, the message, 'With love from Brighton', runs right through the stick of rock from beginning to end. The trouble is that sometimes the message at the heart of a person contains anything but love.

This imprinting of our life by messages from the past was first clarified for the general public by Eric Berne in *Games People Play*. (More recently Thomas Harris has elaborated 'life positions' in *I'm OK, You're OK*.) If our lives really were like cucumbers or a stick of rock, then we would have to accept our lot and make the best of it. *The good news is that the pattern can be changed, the message can be rewritten.* The processes outlined in this book turn the word 'problem' into 'opportunity'.

This kind of change requires a commitment on the part of two people and sometimes a whole group, to be involved in a process of discovery, a way of healing. There are five main steps to be discerned:

1. What is the matter? I need to speak about what my apparent problem is. Why am I unhappy? What is it that I

* See Glossary (p. 182).

want, but cannot have? What seems to happen with monot-
onous regularity and I have no power to prevent? I speak it
out. (How many times have you said to yourself, 'If only I
could find someone who would really understand me'?) A
good listener opens the door. See Appendix 1 for a firsthand
account of this process.

2.   How do I stop myself getting what I want? How do
I resist all offers of help? How do I systematically break my
good resolutions? (How will I try to stop you releasing me
now?) I discover my resistances, compulsions, defences,
ways of suppressing my real needs. It is a very salutary
surprise – even shock – to discover that responsibility for the
muddle I'm in lies in my own hands. Normally, I just don't
see it that way! A good counsellor does not allow me to
bamboozle myself any more.

3.   This brings us to the impasse. This is the point at
which I am stuck, I cannot or will not go through. I need
all your skills, encouragement and sometimes pushing to
move me, provided I am willing, through that difficult place.
If I am unwilling of course, none of these efforts will help
in the slightest and I shall do several more laps of my circuit
of complaint, depression or illness before approaching this
impasse again. But if I take you seriously: if I trust you when
you say 'can't' means 'won't', if I take a risk, the amazing
breakthrough begins. A good therapist will steer me through
the most risky scenario.

4.   I have come through the difficulty, I have expressed
the feeling, recalled the memory, relived the encounter and
done whatever was necessary to push through. Now I need
help to assimilate what has happened, to receive the blessing
and the healing on the other side of the apparent obstacle.
Please pray with me, I need to find acceptance and grace in
my new, vulnerable position. A loving, accepting group will
nurture my new life and give me strength.

5.   The unbelievable has happened and I need to live my
life in this new perspective. It means renewing my mind –
many of my mental attitudes hitherto may have been based
on negative judgments about myself and others. These need
to be realigned with the reality that I can live as a free person,

that I can accept citizenship of God's Kingdom. In shorthand the new perception is 'I'm OK – You're OK'. A broad-spectrum fellowship or church will integrate my new possi-bilities with the wider world.

It must have taken the Israelites a major mental adjustment once they had crossed the River Jordan to settle down in their land of promise, still with skirmishes and battles, but secure in the belief that they belonged here, it was their land. In the same way our ingrained attitudes can change and become life-enhancing. But we have to work at it.

This process of renewing mental attitudes is sometimes called 'rescripting'. The messages which motivated us from the past, whether they come from the cellar or from the attic, were powerful, they were life tramlines which laid down the course of our lives.

> There was a young man of Siam.
> Who said, 'It's seems that I am,
> A being that moves on predestinate grooves,
> I'm not even a bus, I'm a tram.

The scripts need changing, the tramlines need digging up.

A work of healing is complete when I can live in freedom from the destructive echoes of the past and respond with warmth and clear perception to the circumstances and people of today.

The people you are to meet in this book are gathered into a group. They are all real people with the names changed of course. The group, in fact, is a composite of several groups which have met in the recent past at Scargill House in York-shire. When an individual is invited to 'work' or talks about 'my work' he refers to that period of time which he has asked for to bring his own concerns to the attention of the group and, more specifically, to engage in a dialogue with me as facilitator, with the understanding that I will help him to discover within himself the solution which lies on the reverse side of the problem he presents.

Various methods are employed in making this discovery. Gestalt techniques predominate and these are spelled out in detail in the teaching-box at the end of each chapter. There is some deliberate mystification in the use of this German word. No single English word really captures the meanings which have gathered around it. The nearest is 'whole' and if we stay with '*working-together-towards-wholeness*' as a definition of Gestalt therapy we have made a good start. In the picture of the House-in-which-we-live we have a very simple map of the personality and in the concept of movement between attic, living-room and cellar we have outlined a possibility for dialogue, family conference and significant change in the balance-of-power. This is what we are about: a *process* of inner healing and growth by means of rapid change of internal-dynamics. The ways in which this is brought about involve the techniques and concepts known collectively as 'Gestalt'. These are calculated to enable me to speak directly, to stay in touch with my feelings, to use my body-language in discovering my truth, to avoid my avoidances and other defensive ploys, to separate out my interlocking ideas or confused feelings, to demonstrate unmistakably the place at which I feel stuck and also the way in which I 'stick' myself; to take responsibility for my predicament instead of blaming others, and to ask for the help I need in such a way that it is forthcoming.

The 'meetings' which take place in the living-room are often explosive, sometimes joyful, sometimes sad, always deeply moving. Things change by means of direct and vivid dialogue. Things change for good. 'Gestalt' provides the tools-of-the-trade. In *Christian* Gestalt the Holy Spirit provides the power and the skill to use them aright.

Petrushka Clarkson, in a recent book (*Gestalt Counselling in Action*, Sage Books 1989), finds the task of definition equally elusive:

> The aim of the Gestalt approach is for a person to discover, explore and experience his or her own shape, pattern or wholeness. Analysis may be a part of the process but the aim of Gestalt is the integration of all disparate parts. In this way people can let themselves become totally what they already are *and* what they potentially can become. This fullness of experience can

then be available to them both in the course of their life and in the experience of a single moment . . . Gestalt is above all about the whole – smells, tastes, intuitions, the surrounding environment, the historical context. And all of these co-exist like an excellent poem where-in which the artistry is never fully discovered, yet all the symbols and words, and cadences and shapes inter-weave in a tapestry vibrating with life and tragedy and humour.

For more about origins and philosophy of Gestalt see Appendix 2 and for a step by step description of the therapy task see Chapter 11.

In the episodes which follow other styles of work are also encountered – reflective listening, primal integration, resting-in-the-Spirit, prayer-counselling, visualisation and the use of spiritual gifts: a glossary includes these terms (pp. 182–5).

Do I need this healing? Does everybody need it? If the questions are still in your mind please refer again to Appendix 1, 'Please hear what I'm NOT saying' (pp. 177–9).

At the end of each chapter I have included a section called 'Bringing it Home'. You may like to use these questions as part of a personal, healing journey through the various chapters.

The Scripture passages chosen to follow this are there as a commentary on the work described in the chapter. Looking at it another way, the work in the chapter could be described as a commentary on the truth enshrined in the words of Scripture. How can these verses best be used, having read the chapter and thought about the questions? I suggest the following guidelines for your meditation.

1.   What does this passage say about God?

2.   In the light of this chapter what does it say about human nature?

3.   What does it say to *me* in the light of my answers to the questions above?

4.   Visualise Jesus meeting the needs you know you have. Thank him in anticipation of changes.

May those Scriptures, and the prayer that follows, come

alive for you in a new way, and may these pages be full of the comfort – and the discomfort – of the Holy Spirit, for you. And so to meet Tim, the first member of our group to offer to work.

FURTHER READING

Clinical Theology by Frank Lake, abridged by Martin Yeomans (DLT 1986). A digest of Dr Lake's early work on personality disorders. Not for beginners. Technical language but brilliant interface of human need and God's gospel resources.

Healing Adventure by Anne White (Arthur James 1969). A simple introduction to Inner Healing.

Games People Play by Eric Berne (Penguin 1970). A classic, from which the school of Transactional Analysis has sprung.

I'm OK, You're OK by Thomas Harris (Pan books 1973). Easy to read, easy to remember. Check out your own 'life-position' with different people! A simplification of Eric Berne's work.

Listening to Others by Joyce Huggett (Hodder 1988). Joyce's very popular sequel to best-seller *Listening to God*.

Swift to Hear by Michael Jacobs (SPCK 1985). Useful training exercises and role-plays.

Chapter Two

TIM'S STORY: THE MAN WHO RAN AWAY

MANY OF US live with fear as a constant companion. Perhaps we can't imagine what life would be like without it. Our many phobias often have deep unconscious causes. I believe the deepest root-fear is that of annihilation. Fear of death is often at the bottom of a whole list of terrors and dreads in our lives. According to the writer of Hebrews it puts us into '*life-long bondage*' (2:15).

To break the bondage we need to turn and face the fears.

Our anxieties have been described as 'mental rehearsals for disaster and catastrophe'. To face these fantasies head on is to discover that they don't actually happen, and to disperse the tension. Tim's story illustrates poignantly the possibilities of freedom and love which lie beyond the fear-barrier.

It was good to hear Peter's voice again on the telephone after all these years. He and I had shared in the early days of building up a Prayer Counselling Ministry in this country and had learned much together from Anne White.

'I have this new Curate', said Peter. 'It seems he was very depressed when he was in business, he left and trained for the Ministry, which is what he said he always wanted to do. Now he's my Curate and simply not delivering the goods. Some weeks he's fine, but other weeks he's late, and forgetful and evasive. I don't want to come down hard on him, because I know it won't do any good, but I'm at the end of my resources. Do you think you could see him?'

I suggested that he might invite Tim to apply to one of

our Christian Growth weeks and, a month later, here he was walking in through the door. A neatly dressed young man, dark-haired, slimly built, in his early thirties, clean shaven and smiling with bright brown eyes and a demeanour of 'all-there' alertness, the up and coming young executive you might say, if you passed him on a railway platform. His build looked athletic and his manner was, perhaps, a little too assertive. He mingled well with the group at our first meeting, although I noticed one or two keeping their distance from his obvious public school image.

Tim was very well motivated to come to work at Scargill and I noticed by foot-tapping and catching my eye during introductions to the group, that he was likely to be the one to start this evening. His work began in a familiar enough way, to one with an organised life and tidy mind. He had programmed the points which he would like to discuss and he even read them out to us. I listened patiently to his intro-ductory remarks, with their self-depreciatory tone, until he said, 'It is as if people are chasing me.' Then I homed in to follow the development of a kind of day-dream which ensued. Tim's imagination was powerfully presenting in a kind of motion picture the truth he needed to tell. (Dreams at night often perform the same function.) He found himself running away through woods and out across open country.

As you read what follows, allow yourself in imagination to join that group as I retell the experience in the present tense. Notice the difference in atmosphere and attention when I ask Tim to stop and face his pursuers. It marks the turning-point in this session and a turning-point in his life. I intervene at three points in the work – to encourage fight rather than flight. Here is the dialogue which took place:

IAN: 'I can see you have begun to programme your work with us tonight.'

TIM: 'I'm afraid you won't like me. You won't like me if you know how angry I can be. What I really feel and think won't be very original.'

          Tim is smiling as he speaks.

IAN: 'What's behind your smile?'

TIM: 'I'm feeling frightened but I smile, rather like a manipulating child, my pulse is racing and my mouth is dry. It's as if people are chasing me, and I have just stopped. I can't tell if they are still chasing me because of the noise of my racing pulse.'

IAN: 'Who are they?'

TIM: 'People I hide from. I don't want them to know what I'm really like. I seem to be running through this wood with brambles tearing at my clothing. I'm out now in a clearing in the sunlight, but while it will be easier for me, it will be easier for them too.'

IAN: 'Risk hiding behind a tree and being found. Let your hands shake as they want to.'

Tim is visibly moved by the experience which is beginning. The group of people surrounding him seem to have faded away. He is vividly in touch with the scene he is describing. His hands and arms begin to tremble. The shaking and trembling move Tim to tears.

IAN: 'What are your tears?'

TIM: 'The tears and trembling have my name – Tim, they are me.'

IAN: 'Describe your mental picture, what's happening now?'

TIM: 'There's a wide valley beyond the wood, devoid of people but cultivated. The people chasing me have vanished. How have they been silenced? They have silenced themselves, but they must be there.'

IAN: 'Go and look for them.'

Come on out

This causes Tim more tears and trembling; he turns, 'Where are you?' he shouts. 'Here I am, I'm not running away from you.' 'I'm Tim, so where and who are you?' (Pause) 'They are all the bosses I have ever had. All men, they all look surprised as they approach, they can't believe they are frightening me. Father won't come out. Come on out, Dad, you don't know any of them, and yet without you, none of them would be here.' Tim's voice falters.

The group seems restive, perhaps disappointed that Father won't appear. I decide to change tack and refer Tim to his posture.

IAN: 'What are you feeling in your body now, notice your shoulders are stiff, your upper lip tight, your hands clenched.'

Tim's whole body language speaks of fear and impending conflict. It is as if he is at the point of confrontation which his whole life pattern has sought to avoid. But the group and I are seeking to do the opposite, to promote it!

IAN: 'Relax a little, you don't have to run away from him, let him emerge. Can you see him?'

TIM: 'Yes, I can see Father now.'

He begins speaking quietly and tentatively to his father.

TIM: 'Life was always a struggle for you, and you always said you wouldn't allow it to be for your children, *but you let me know this*, so it was a struggle in a different way. My struggle is to find the things to hide behind. It would be much easier to be myself rather than constantly having to pretend.'

IAN: 'Can you be yourself with him now?'

Tim smiles.

TIM: 'I've done it before, but what's the point?'

IAN: 'It's the point of your being here this week.'

TIM: 'I'm only real with two people in the world, but I want to share and you're in the way Dad, so I can't communicate with hundreds of others.'

Tim begins to explain this at length to Dad and talks about his feelings of being hammered, beaten and paralysed at home and how this seems to affect all his relationships with older people.

TIM: 'I know this hurts you, but that's because you hurt me.'

IAN: 'But you must hurt him to be free.'

TIM: 'My head aches.'

Tim describes a dull pain. 'The sort of ache which you

have by trying to concentrate too hard.'

A quick glance round the group reveals faces which show a puzzled, beaten (even bored) look. We are all following very closely and find ourselves being subtly drawn in to this impasse of Tim's own making. A change of posture is overdue!

Stand up to him

IAN: 'Stand up on your own two feet. Stand up to him.'
        And Tim does this with hands on his hips.

TIM: 'I'm not sure what I'm more afraid of, your words or your physical presence. Oh I know, it's your temper. I really run a mile from that. I've seen what it can do and what it's done to me. I've got it too. Your temper means I daren't have an opinion for myself. If you disagree with it, you will hit me verbally. But I don't let you know that you've hit me and crushed me. I defer to you and shut up.'

Tim is still 'parleying' – analysing, wondering how far it is safe to go in this strange new situation. He is after all confronting his fear (in the shape of Father) for the first time. Ian intervenes, suggesting that Tim moves across the room and 'becomes' his father. Discoveries of unsuspected truth are often made by role-playing *both* sides of a dialogue.

IAN: 'Take time to get into the role of Dad. What would he respond?'

Tim speaks as Dad.

TIM/   'I don't know what you mean, I've always treated
DAD: you boys fairly. I knew you were the sensitive one, but you have always seemed so distant with me. I can't get near you, I often wonder what you are thinking of me and since you've gone into the Church, well I sometimes feel quite apprehensive of you. But I don't want to hurt or crush you . . . good heavens, what nonsense, it's the last thing I want to do.'

Tim changes back and becomes himself. I ask him to make

a definite physical step across every time he changes role so that he is clear, and it's obvious to us, which part he is playing.

TIM: 'You know deep down what you have done, although you deny it and you can't believe you're going on doing it.'

IAN: 'You can't change *him*, Tim. No amount of reasoning will change him.'

TIM: 'But *I* can change, I want a real relationship with you. I want to talk about everything under the sun. Not just what you want to talk about. I can hear your voice in mine when I'm talking to others and I don't want that part of you. I want a mind of my own, although it may not be right, but at least it is my own. You've stopped me, you *do* know you have.' He speaks with rising strength. 'You *have* stopped me.'

IAN: 'Make a straight demand.'

TIM: 'I, I'm going to make a demand. I demand that we tell each other the truth.'

IAN: 'Tell him something that's true.'

TIM: 'You frighten me.'

IAN: 'Dad doesn't know how he's frightened you.'

TIM: 'You frighten me by your words, your physical presence and by your absence. Because your parents took it out on you, why take it out on me? What really frightens me, is that I'm going to do the same with my children, or that you will.'

Action

At this point I produce a large cushion and an encounter bat. This is a truncheon-like weapon made of strengthened rubber padded with foam. At this point I deliberately move Tim from talk into action to express more fully and completely the frustration and anger which lurk behind his fear. I ask Tim to kneel in front of the cushion and bring the bat down heavily on the cushion as he speaks to his father. There is much grunting, groaning and puffing as Tim moves into action, expressing his feelings through the bat and the cushion.

TIM: 'I hate you. I hate the way you crush me, I'm not going to stand it any longer. You embarrass me when you spend money on me, it does not mean you can have my love. You are not to discipline my children! It's my job, keep your hands off! My love cannot be bought and what happens is only the opposite, hate. I feel I have got to give you value for money. I hate doing this, but I'm bloody well going to do it.'

(Many heavy bangs on the cushion.) Tim sits back exhausted with the effort and looks at the result of his work.

TIM: 'There's still a person there and he's not destroyed. He knows what I feel now.'

Suddenly with tears streaming down his face, Tim lunges forward, grabs the cushion and hugs it.

TIM: 'I love you, in spite of everything.'

Tim's works ends as powerfully as it had begun fearfully. It takes us all by surprise. The group respond with cries of delight and encouragement. Tim rejoins the group in conscious awareness. Somehow we feel that his father now 'belongs' here too.

The name of the game is Risk. Tim's first risk was to face those pursuers who might now discover what he was really like and to face them in the company of the group of people surrounding him. The second risk was to face Father and to speak up. The third was to add the whole weight of pent up frustration in a physical way. It was the risk of exposure and vulnerability, which is the first on the road to healing. He took big risks in his imaginary journey and, lest the word 'imagination' should convey the sense of something ephemeral or intangible, may I say that the encounter between Tim and his father was the most real thing in the room. To face up to someone, or to go on avoiding the issue . . . we all know the dilemma. In facing up to Father, Tim effectively defused the fear which had been chasing him.

I intervened at several points; first, I asked him to face his pursuers instead of running away across the open country. His pursuers were his fears and all healing begins with facing up to fears and moving out of the place of hiding or running away. There is a necessary turning-point. The second turning-point occurred when I invited him to stand up to his father. He quite literally stood up and had it out with the old man. He got it off his chest, where of course it had been doing him no good. Then, I invited him to become his father and feel the dilemma which *he* was in, not being able to communicate and not being able to understand his son and feeling quite sure that the accusations against him were grossly exaggerated if not altogether false.

I needed to convince Tim that he would never change his father, 'but', said Tim, '*I* can change', and this was his third turning-point in the work. He then demonstrated how he could change by making straight requests and demands. He said clearly what he wanted. It was significant that he needed to stand up on his feet. When I asked the group at that point, 'What is missing from Tim's anatomy?' several people spotted that his feet and legs were entirely immobile, he might have been in a wheelchair. It was only the top part of his body which was animated at all. In asking him to stand up, we were going for the missing part – recovering the lost part of his anatomy.

He needed no longer to be paralysed in front of his father, he could reverse the decision he had made and abided by for so many years (to defer to the older man's opinions and wishes), without losing respect for him. In fact, no one was more surprised than Tim to discover that, once the new declaration had been made and the hateful feelings expressed, vigorously and violently, but harmlessly upon a large and dusty cushion, he was free to express his love. It is as if the love within us is like a gushing, springing well, but the outlet is often clogged by rocks of hate and resentment, which need to be cleared away, before love can flow again. I do not suggest that such vigorous action be taken in a real-life scenario – too many black eyes would result.

Clearing the air with 'cushion work' is a more productive and effective bit of drama. Once we are sure we have identified the person to whom the negative feeling really belongs, we produce a big cushion and say, 'That is the person, kneel in front and express all the feeling that is now in your fists or in your feet'. The person working is encouraged to punch or kick or use an encounter bat, and with great vigour and determination to express all the feeling that is within them. Most people are surprised and delighted to discover that once this negative feeling is expressed, they are then free to enter other feelings, which may follow, such as remorse, sadness, even fear and sometimes the joy of reconciliation. Then forgiveness becomes possible. Thus it is that one of the very first steps in Healing is the authentic expression of feelings towards the person to whom they belong. In Tim's case, his anger and resentment were only turning inwards and causing him to feel 'flat', in other words 'depressed'. It really 'belonged' out there between himself and Father.

I noticed in his script* references to himself, doing things he hated or saying things which sounded 'just like his father', and many of us who have children will recognise this. It seems that our parents pattern us with a kind of hidden watermark, which is there seemingly indelibly, so that we repeat their methods and mistakes down the generations; they are, after all, the only models we had. Significantly in Tim's work, however, he made a new decision. He would break decisively with the past. He would refuse the pattern of acting 'victim' to his father's persecution and domination. He would speak on the adult level to him and take the consequences. This is what healing is all about. It is a process of re-learning and renewing the mind. Tim can consciously make a decisive break with the past and in the power of the Holy Spirit and the strength of his armour, he can maintain a new stance before his father. Tim's decision was to stop running away, to level with and speak face to face with him. He will now maintain a vigilant and adult-to-adult relationship, which will give him self-respect and put any

* See Appendix 2 (pp. 180–1) for definition of 'script'.

anger or irritation 'out there' where it belongs, instead of 'in here'.

Tim finished his session with a personal prayer for courage and truthfulness and power to change. It is important to be specific in such a prayer, turning away from those 'devices and desires of our own hearts' which we have used to protect ourselves. He repented of three things (1) the fear involved in running away, (2) the false belief that it was the only course of action possible and (3) the deception involved in hiding his real opinions and feelings. When we settle for a quiet life and hide our real feelings, a deception is always involved. We are telling less than the truth, and keeping a mask in place. Repentance is needed and a new way of being real has to be learned if we wish to recover our mental health and peace. In so far as Tim's relationship with his father was a contributory cause of his depression, and in so far as Tim can assimilate this work and his new decisions into life, and relationships with his 'superiors' he will have no need to feel depressed.

NEW TO YOU? A METHOD-LEARNING BOX FOR COUNSELLORS

The House

In terms of the 'House' illustration of Chapter 1, Tim had a lack of balance and no freedom to move. Loud, dominant commands were coming from parents in the attic, whilst cowering in the cellar crouched his frightened child. Incidentally the child may spend a lot of time colluding with the angry shouting, telling himself, 'That's right, I *am* disobedient, my views *don't* matter, I really *should* do what I'm told and believe what I'm told.' A system is set up which is bound to produce depression and paralysis in the living-room. It will go on doing so until decisively broken.

The Voices

The 'voices' are internalised. It is as if Tim has swallowed his father whole: so, to put it right do the opposite, *externalise* the offending voice. Put it literally 'out-there' on a cushion and then we can hear, and even see, the true process. We must separate before we can integrate.

Opposites

If the avoidance is running away (flight) then encourage the *opposite* to take place i.e. confrontation (fight). Tim was not only asked to stop running, but actively to *look for* his pursuers. The dialogue-method reveals accurately and surely the real dynamics. Avoid interpretations and self-analytical comments from the person working. Tim intellectualised at times, leading us all on a (boring) 'head' trip.

Body Language

Watch body language at these times. It speaks louder than words. Tim's inert and passive lower limbs gave the clue to what he really needed to do (stand up to Father). His clenched fists showed what he wanted to do. He was encouraged to *act* the whole scenario out in dramatic form. Talking *about* it would have been more 'gossip' and produced no results.

BRINGING IT HOME

1. When you feel depressed or flat, who is it that you are really resenting? Search around until you find '*who*' rather than '*what*' the matter is!
2. What will it cost to stand and face up to this person? What's in it for you to keep things as they are? (Anything for a quiet life?)
3. How do you find you stop yourself changing things? What do you choose now to do about it?
4. Is it Christian to stand up for myself?

SCRIPTURE

2 Timothy 1:7–8 (RSV)
For God did not give us a spirit of timidity but a spirit of power and love and self-control. Do not be ashamed then of testifying to our Lord, nor of me his prisoner, but take your share of suffering for the gospel in the power of God.

PRAYER

Dear Lord, grant us courage to change the things we can change. Grant us serenity to accept the things we cannot change and grant us wisdom to know the difference. Amen.

FURTHER READING

Emotionally Free by Rita Bennett (Kingsway 1982), esp. pp. 48–58 which covers these topics: Do you need soul healing?; Prose poem 'sole talk'; What soul-healing isn't; Did Jesus pray this way?; Faults need healing; A checklist for soul-healing; Does everyone need specific prayer help?

Chapter Three

JANE'S STORY: THE WOMAN IN THE DOCK

MANY PEOPLE battle with feelings of inferiority. The notorious 'inferiority complex' is a bit like an elephant – hard to describe, but we know one when we see one (or feel its effects!). This is the true story of Jane whose 'complex' has all the weight and power to crush of an elephant. Long ago Jane had given up the unequal struggle and had settled for inner condemnation, a kind of life-sentence. The accusing voices were so strong. The judge's verdict seemed so right. As the psalmist once concluded, '*I am a worm and no man*'. I deserve only to be put away, kept under lock and key, perhaps even exterminated. This is extreme. But, as Shakespeare reminds us, 'conscience doth make cowards of us all'. We *all* have to come to terms with an inner dialogue which includes a voice from the attic – often critical, sometimes harsh and condemning. The kind of terms we come to will influence our ability fully to accept the gospel and to enjoy life.

In the work which follows we separate out the voices within Jane's head. There is a transmitter of strident accusing messages which we call Top-Dog. These instructions and 'life-sentences' correspond with the 'voices-from-the-attic' identified in Chapter 1. Jane has her own short-hand: she ruefully christens her punisher 'The Bitch'. The Receiver, Jane's weaker self, we call her 'Under-Dog'!

Jane really believed she owed the world an apology for being here at all. She lived a divided life, outwardly calm and competent, inwardly condemned and collapsing. My main message to her was: '*You are punishing yourself, why not stop? Choose to do what you really want to do.*'

A vicar's wife from a Midland town, she looked youngish-middle-aged, obviously used to taking the strain of pastoral problems in parish life. She was respected for her practical wisdom and ability to cope. No one would guess that *she* had any problems. She dressed neatly in a tweed skirt, white blouse and dark blue cardigan. Her demeanour was kindly, but slightly forbidding. The group seemed comforted by her reassuring motherly presence and obviously concerned for her as her agitation began to become apparent.

I asked her to play different roles to dramatise what was going on. This was enacted in terms of a court scene with a severe judge and a prisoner in the dock. The inner voice spoke accusation, judgement and condemnation continuously. Having no control over them she therefore believed that they must be right, and felt alienated and excluded from the warmth, company and intimacy for which she longed. For the judge figure we use the shorthand 'Top-Dog' and the part of herself in the dock we will call 'Under-Dog'. In some shape or form all of us are familiar with the inner dialogue between these two protagonists. The work with Jane depended on separating out these elements and discovering what is really going on inside . . . her 'process'. We relied heavily on participation by the group both at the beginning and the end of the work. The turning-point came when I challenged the assertions made by Top-Dog on Jane's behalf. You will notice how she ignored my challenge at first. Jane's Top-Dog gave the impression of being the size and weight of the world on her shoulders, and absolutely invincible. The first result of the work is that she now perceives it as the size of a hazelnut which could easily be slipped into her handbag. Here are extracts from the dialogue which took place.

The great controller

JANE: 'I am aware that I have deep problems and that I
          have spent most of my life preventing people from
          reaching them. I hope that I won't prevent you, I
          really very much want to. I have deep feelings.
          My life consists of controlling me. In controlling
          me I control you.'

She bites her thumb-nail. I invite her to reverse the '*con-
trolled-controlling*' position by moving out of her chair and
standing on a line between two carpets. A change of posture
can free us for a change of attitude.

JANE: 'I'm on the edge. I feel that I am standing on a
          line: which way am I going to fall off it? What's
          at stake? If I step back and keep safe then nobody
          will find out what's bothering me, but if I step
          forward I will get out of control, people will find
          out about me and I have had troubles with that in
          the past. I think that I am afraid of admitting to
          myself that I am the judge of me. It will hurt me
          so much.'

IAN: 'What do you want from us now?'

JANE: 'What I want from the group is not to reject me.
          If I do little bits I can sense reactions. That's how
          to find out by doing little things that don't really
          matter.'

IAN: 'Are you here to do something that doesn't really
          matter? I suggest that you say to the group, "If
          you really knew me, you wouldn't like me." Do
          the rounds of the group, make eye contact with
          each member in turn and ask them if they would
          reject you.'

Jane follows these instructions and seems reassured by the
members of the group. This is an important step. Jane is
prepared to take risks with a new vulnerability and needs to
know she has the full support of the group.

IAN: 'Would you like to play the judge? Look, stand
          on this chair and look down and judge yourself.'

I place a cushion on the floor in front of the chair and Jane

climbs on to the chair. I am now inviting her to identify
fully with the condemning voice. It helps literally to 'look
down' on herself – now represented by the cushion.

Judgement from above

IAN: 'Judge Jane in the inmost parts.'

JANE: 'I'm blocking by going blank. I do want to do it.'
   She addresses the cushion in a calm, steady voice.

JANE (as Top-Dog):   'You are an absolute idiot, you never
                     get anything right, you mess up everything and
                     hurt everybody.'

IAN: 'Can you say it with feeling?'

JANE: 'No I can't.'

IAN: 'Do you want to say it with feeling?'

JANE: 'No.'

IAN: 'Notice how you stop yourself contacting the feel-
          ing. You have given us the label but not the
          parcel.'

   I cannot 'make' Jane do anything. I can only bring to her
attention her 'process' which is to stop herself doing what
she has said she *wants* to do! She needed me to repeat my
comment and paused to take it in.

JANE   'Yes, therefore my reaction is to turn away. I'm
(T.D.):   not angry, it's futile, there's no aggression, she's
          weakened enough, she's revolting. Ugh.'

IAN: 'Name the feeling that grunt stands for.'

JANE   'It's revulsion. Let's go away, close down the
(T.D.):   shop, back out, disappear, exterminate – you
          deserve obliteration.'

IAN: 'Can you say from the chair, "I exterminate you"?'

JANE   'I want to exterminate you, you're useless.'
(T.D.):

IAN: 'Try the word "contemptible". So you're a
          mighty powerful lady as you address your congre-
          gation of one. Do you have a reply to your judge
          from down below? She's waiting to exterminate
          you!'

Jane climbs down.

JANE: 'No, I, I want to go with it – the extermination.'

Alone again

She walks determinedly out of the room. The group sits in shocked silence, no one moves. Jane has acted out the 'extermination' by removing herself physically from the room. Again it illustrates one of her life-processes. 'I keep myself safely under control out here, and doing so, I control you.' In a few minutes Elizabeth gets up and goes to look for her. Jane comes back in with Elizabeth explaining that it was all part of the process and she was wanting to be brought back in, but at the same time she says to Liz, 'I felt that you were interfering, I didn't want anyone to be kind.' So Jane confused Liz and all of us with her double-message.

IAN: 'Jane, what *do* you want?'

JANE: 'I want to be alone, it's safer that way, I can get through life. I'm better on my own, there are less complications, less hassles.'

IAN: 'Walk alone round the room, experience how it is better for you on your own.'

JANE: (walking round) 'I'm alone, I like it, it's safe. I do need the group, but not too close.'

IAN: 'How close?'

JANE: 'Not, not into the inner sanctuary.'

IAN: 'I thought I heard you say, "Help me *stop* preventing people getting in" – it's inconsistent, you can't have it both ways.'

Jane responds to this gentle but firm confrontation. She still feels a 'born loser' but she's got guts – she's a trier too! She walks back to her starting line which was in fact a division between two carpets. She stands toeing the line.

JANE: 'I want to go the way that leads to risk, I've been outside the door most of my life, I'm scared stiff as soon as I stand on this line, it's like brick walls, a band of steel. I can stand anywhere else and make a choice, but on this line there's terror, fear is getting out of control, my feelings are taking over.'

IAN: 'The first one is fear. Can you allow it, give it permission to speak?'

JANE: 'Fear, I give you permission to speak. I am afraid of being out of control, I'm afraid of being loved.'

IAN: 'Who by?'

JANE: 'I'm not sure – anyone, but I'm not sure who the real person is. My fears are increasing, I'm afraid when anything is expected of me; of failing; what will happen; I've let people down – friends.'

I interrupt. Jane could easily play me another tape of 'trying and failing'.

She obviously has a lot of fear of the threatening Top-Dog in herself. But I don't want her to wallow in it or to allow herself to be pushed out again. I am more than ready for battle with this 'space-invader' so I challenge her sharply to fight back.

IAN: 'You have spent your life agreeing with someone who says you are useless.'

JANE: 'But those friends have given me something; I have nothing to give back, there's nothing that I *can* give back, there's nothing that I can give you Ian. I'm finding it difficult, I want to please you. She, that one on the chair [points to Top-Dog place], she told me I'd messed it all up by not coming back in.'

Counter-attack

IAN: '*I want you to live*, my only expectation is that you would answer *her*. Answer Top-Dog back. Up to now you have obeyed and colluded with her. You feel she is right, you've spent your life agreeing with someone who says you are worthless and wants to exterminate you.'

JANE: 'I agree with it now.'

IAN: '*When are you going to repent, because it is a pack of lies*? When you say these things you are lying and destroying yourself. That's the work of the devil. When are you going to believe the gospel at last? Right now is the time.'

Jane stepped forward at this challenge. She crossed the line on which she had been standing.

IAN: 'I'd like a re-run of the earlier scene, without the walk-out bit.' He points at Top-Dog's chair. 'Tell her to "come off it".'

JANE: 'I don't *feel* it.'

IAN: 'Of course you don't because she has had her way for so long. Tell her, "Okay, who are you running me around? Who do you think you are up there? I'm not going to allow you to push me around, squash me and wipe me out any longer!" Can you dialogue with her, get a hold of her supremacy? You need to come to a place of believing that she's a liar.'

I am now taking sides, urgently and directively. I want to reinforce whatever strength Jane has left in her Under-Dog to get this matter settled once and for all.

Jane pauses to think and assimilates this instruction. Seeing her situation in a flash she responds firmly.

JANE: 'You can just get lost, you've ruled for too long and there's no way that I'm going to stay under your control. You've lost control, you've lost the right to speak, it's all lies you've kept me under for so long.'

She turns to the group.

JANE: 'I think it's right, it's been done, it's been said, I mean it. There's a choice and "the bitch" has to go, she's lost her place, she's lost the authority and power because I've taken it away.'

Cut down to size

IAN: 'Top-Dogs have their uses. Get back on the chair and see how she has received what you said.'

Jane complies.

JANE   'As Top-Dog I believe she means what she says.
(T.D.):   Jane, do you realise what this means? [I want to
           get down and answer.]'

Jane climbs down from the position on the chair to the
floor and answers.

JANE: 'If you say that you don't know how much bond-
           age I've been in, you don't know how many times
           I've had to go out of the room and spend my
           life walking alone. If you knew how many years
           you've crippled me you wouldn't question my
           response tonight.'

Then from the chair she says (as T.D.):

           'You're going to feel mighty funny, you're going
           to miss me. I'll just watch and wait, you can't
           keep it up.'

As Jane speaks her left hand is clenched, making wringing
movements. I give her a towel.

IAN: 'Wring it so tightly that it disintegrates in the
           middle. That's it.'

Jane wrings the towel with great energy.

JANE: 'Top-Dog, this is how I want to wring your neck.
           Exterminator I've got you.'

The group is visibly relieved. Jane seems to have saved
her life from extinction.

Jane shakes the towel out and puts it over the chair.

JANE: 'As I put the towel over her Top-Dog reduced in
           size to a small nut. I'll just smother her and go.'

IAN: 'Well, it's no more than she deserves, but can
           you renegotiate something with her? You certainly
           don't want "the bitch" in full power, but what
           kind of Top-Dog *do* you need? Can she become
           an encourager, can she learn to approve of you?'

JANE: 'No she can't, she's under the towel, she's gone
           down in size, she's a small nut under the towel.
           I'm not going to ever let you get to that size and
           proportion again; I've seen you reduced, you're
           no longer significant. Because you're so small I
           probably won't hear your lies. I can speak very

quietly, I can grind you up with my foot. Before you were so big [pauses, musing].'

IAN: 'What's happening?'

I notice Jane's momentum begin to flag: she sits down turning her back on the towel.

JANE: 'I'm thinking about John writing, I'm thinking about the tape, the old pattern in me. Oh dear, I've done it again.'

IAN: 'What?'

Jane goes on to tell us that she's feeling distress. She's upset that now everybody will *know* what she is really like. She has expressed very strong and angry feeling in wringing the towel. Her experience has taught her that this brings dire consequences and she now begins to expect 'something awful to happen'. She experiences embarrassment alternating with a determination not to go back on what *has* happened.

She is like a horse that shows signs of refusing the jumps, so I put her head straight at the difficulty again, saying in effect, 'Do the very thing you're afraid of . . . now.' I ask her to move round the group, standing before each one in turn and say something that is true and from the heart about their relationship. I ask her to do the same for me. With a mischievous nudge in the ribs she says, 'It's lovely that you don't give up on me . . . you don't let me off the hook.'

In conclusion I invite the group gently to express affirmation and affection for Jane. She is prepared to take another risk in vulnerability – to receive and to believe in their love.

Jane completes the task. The bell goes for lunch and I close the session.

It seemed like a completed piece of work and in one sense it was. In another sense, the work had only just begun as Jane revealed in a subsequent letter.

W hat impressed me about her work was the enormous, dominant strength of Top-Dog or in Jane's own succinct phrase, 'the bitch'. It had power to condemn her and keep her isolated from people, it prevented her from sharing her real self, even from her nearest and dearest.

We all need a critical function with which to evaluate our own performance and that of others. We all need the capacity to question our own motives, to be shrewd and discerning rather than blind and gullible, but in Jane's case that faculty had grown out of all proportion, it is as if the only thing she received from her parents and from many teachers was a constant stream of criticism; her child mind had said, 'If you put me down like that for so long, I must be bad and I'll have to believe it's true.' The critical voices had been internalised, taken right into her inmost being, there to continue a merciless war of threats and accusations until she lived in a constant state of fear and collapse on the inside. Frank Lake called such accusing voices 'the human demonic'. She could never ask for or obtain what she wanted in life, because it would always be 'wrong'.

The first step in emotional release is to dethrone and depose the reigning monarch – the critical Top-Dog – and this Jane effectively accomplished in the work. She also began to take courage and trust the group. The first interaction with the group was to be assured that she would not be rejected whatever happened. The work finished with a similar round-up, this time both to express her feelings and to receive their appreciation and affection. The latter needed to be done with great care and sensitivity lest Jane be overwhelmed and retreat into the security of her isolation and unbelief.

Having spotted the demonic voices within her and called them the liars and destroyers that they really are, her next step spiritually will be to repent of the sin of believing these negative judgements for so long, for they contradict the revealed Word of God. It is extraordinary how many of us manage to entertain and nourish such voices within us even though with our conscious mind we welcome the Word of God and believe ourselves to be saved, redeemed and members of the Body of Christ. These messages should not co-exist, they are in direct conflict. The conflict will give us no peace until the affair is sorted out.

The stakes were high for Jane and a lot of resistance had to be overcome before she would work at identifying 'the bitch' and her messages. There was even more resistance to the suggestion that these messages were lies and that she had in effect been believing lies. Once she had received this information and understood it there was no stopping her in the new process of turning the tables. But in order to do this she had to become aware of the vicious circle of condemnation she was living in. This 'circuitry' would ensure a continuous repeat pattern throughout life. Unless interrupted and changed with some vigour, it becomes a life-sentence. For Jane it was a self-destructive process. Most of us live so closely caught up within our 'process' that we do not notice it, far less have the opportunity to change it. This opportunity comes, as it came for Jane, when we can separate out the voices, in this case Top-Dog/Under-Dog (the bitch and her victim).

GETTING THE HANG OF IT? SOME HINTS ON THE METHODS USED WITH JANE FOR COUNSELLORS AND THERAPISTS

Jane is locked into a place of hellish condemnation.

The Action-plan thus becomes:
1. Separate.   (Top-Dog/Under-Dog)
2. Negotiate.   (A new 'deal' is possible)
3. Integrate.   (Pray, visualise and work this into life)

1. Using Dialogue
We need to separate out the parts of ourselves into their polarities. We need to allow them to dialogue one with the other so that we can hear the content and power of what is happening.
2. Then realising that these are interrelated parts of our own inner selves we do something about it. We redress the balance, we re-educate the parts of ourselves which are getting out of hand, too dominant or too submissive. We do this in the light of the Word of God which brings freedom to captives and sight to hitherto blind eyes. There is a new

order in our 'house' and the living-room is more spacious, comfortable and quieter!

3. The final stage of integration comes when the new-covenant-within-us becomes effective as we assimilate the work into our daily living. This new agreement, or 'truce', is the first step in thinking with the mind of Christ. He has done it for us 'once for all' in history and eternally. According to Romans 10:4, *Christ is the end of the Law* (Top-Dog) which has held us in bondage to failure and punishment. Christ gives us grace to live by faith according to the Word of God. He sets us free to respond to his commandments in spontaneity and from motives of love. Prayer is needed for Jane that the Word of God will now be given its proper authority. Top-Dog is dethroned. The sting is drawn.

Acting Out
Notice how the helping process is made easier by dramatising, by using chairs, lines on the floor, by moving about, and encouraging expression of feeling by e.g. wringing a towel. Reservoirs of stored-up feeling may be drained by watching for body-language clues and by providing equipment with which to work it all out. The drama within is now 'acted out' for all to see and for Jane to understand.

Frustration
When Jane reaches the place of difficulty (impasse), I prevent her avoiding the issue. I point out her process, and keep re-addressing the central issue. I frustrate all attempts to play weak or fearful or to control the group, and encourage her, in her strength, to overcome.

Confront
her contradictions or inconsistencies. I point out emphatically that she wants to be free, to allow people to know her, to find warmth and love, *but* she will persist in believing 'the bitch' and kowtowing to her. Jane blocks herself and needs a big challenge to repentance in order to

rearrange the interior dialogues so that she hears truth instead of lies.

Use the Group
They are generous in resources of warmth and support, and can be relied upon to spot a person's delaying or controlling tactics.

Respect
the power of fantasy. It may sound like a daydream or imagination, but such imagery has power to motivate and control lives (e.g. the hazelnut picture).

BRINGING IT HOME

How often do I keep quiet rather than say what I'm really feeling? Always? Sometimes? Hardly ever? Never?
Look at each significant relationship in your life in the light of this.
If I persist in accusing, judging and condemning myself, whose voice am I choosing to believe and agree with? (Rev. 12:9.)
Is it possible to believe one thing and to live another?
Listen to yourself during the course of a day talking to the children or subordinates. How much of your output sounds like Top-Dog?
How did Jesus deal decisively with '*that Accuser of the brethren*', Rev. 12:10?
Can you insert the personal pronoun (me, my) in the passage which follows?

SCRIPTURE

Colossians 2:13b–15 (Phillips Modern English)
God has now made (you) to share in the very life of Christ! He has forgiven you all your sins: Christ has utterly wiped out the

damning evidence of broken laws and commandments which always hung over our heads and has completely annulled it by nailing it over his own head on the cross. And then, having drawn the sting of all the powers ranged against us, he exposed them shattered, empty and defeated, in his final glorious triumphant act!

PRAYER

Lord, help me to cut 'Top-Dog' down to size.
I'm justified by faith in you,
Not by living up to rules and expectations
I've been a fool to believe that accusing voice.
Lord, I want to listen only to you;
Your truth will set me free.

FURTHER READING

A Tool for Christians Books 1 and 2 by Jean Grigor (Morrison) (Dept of Education of the Church of Scotland 1980, 1983). Jean Morrison's user-friendly guide to the Transactional Analysis scene. Of particular relevance to this chapter are Chapters 3 and 7 of Book 1.

Fully Human, Fully Alive by John Powell (Fount Books, Collins 1976).

Why am I afraid to tell you who I am? by John Powell (Fontana 1975). John Powell, an American Catholic priest and pastoral educator, writes with a beautiful lucidity and simplicity about human personality and relationships.

Chapter Four

BOB'S STORY – THE MAN WHO WON'T LISTEN

C. S. LEWIS once wrote in an imaginary obituary, 'She simple *lived* to help other people, you could tell the others by their hunted look'.

If you have been pursued by well-wishers or do-gooders, or if you find someone's presence is enough to make you feel uncomfortable and shut you up like a clam, then follow Bob's story closely. On the other hand you may identify more nearly with Bob, someone who had a compulsive need to help others, and an earnest desire to understand both himself and them.

The episode that follows is full of avoidances – what Eric Berne called 'Games' – playing psychiatry, playing confused, misunderstood, 'hurt'. The good news is that when we stop such tactics because we see and hear what we are doing, then God has a chance to change us and help us grow up.

B ob gave me the feeling that he was talking *at* me rather than *to* me. I began to feel this whenever he approached me outside the group. He was tall, had what Shakespeare would call 'a lean and hungry look'. I began to feel guarded, I did not want to be devoured by him, but he remorselessly sought my attention and poured out his troubles and specu-lations, opinions, faults and questions without waiting for answers or responses. It became clear that he was not in the habit of listening to people, to God or even to himself. Neither did he seem to notice my signs of discomfort and needing to back away. In short he had 'lost' his eyes and his ears.

My purpose in working with Bob was to help him realise this and to begin really to listen and to see himself. He felt like a man with no boundaries, no definition, he did not seem to know where he ended and other people began.

The group was very fond of Bob, but I sensed a wariness of his presence in conversation. People were guarding against his tendency to overwhelm, to take over and to bring an atmosphere of confusion.

The story I am going to tell illustrates a good beginning, a mapping out of the problem. It gives Bob an awareness of what he does and how he does it; in no way does it look at root causes of his inner compulsions – though strong verbal clues are given. In terms of healing it marks the *start* of his journey. We have named the problem, we have heard the Word of the Lord, we have not yet arrived at a healing solution.

Bob is invited to stop rationalising and intellectualising, to stop asking 'why' questions and to allow for a while the other side of his brain to operate, the side that brings pictures and images and conveys another dimension of truth. God wants Bob's energetic analytical mind to rest, to 'be still', (to stop fighting) – and to allow pictures to form. He speaks powerfully through imagery.

You will notice in the first part of the dialogue how Bob longs to understand what is going on. The word 'understand' or similar words occur six times in the first few minutes. I have to use hard and intensive questioning to stop him, to stop his need to 'flood' with explanations and analysis. I ask 'how' questions and refuse to answer his 'why' questions; I attempt to give him focus into the present moment, a 'here and now' focus.

The difficulty Bob is wrestling with at the beginning of his work*-session is his attitude to me. He wants to trust me, but feels offended by my apparent failure to give him the full attention and consideration he needed when trying

---

* 'Work' in this sense is explained towards the end of Chapter 1 (p. 9) and in the Glossary.

to decide whether or not to 'work'. In asking him whether he wanted to start I became confused and baffled by his ambiguous replies. He did and he didn't, and he would like a few things made clear first, and anyway was it right that he should? What did the group feel? Could I guarantee that anything would change? In response I short-circuited the 'waffle' and moved on to someone else who *was* ready to work. Bob was left feeling slightly bruised by this. It emerges in the first part of the dialogue.

A bruised reed?

IAN: 'Bob, what are you aware of today?'

BOB: 'I'm aware of a tiredness, I feel emotionally battered in many ways.'

IAN: 'Where?'

BOB: 'It's to do with what you said about confusion. There are so many situations to react and respond to. I don't understand my response to you, why you didn't understand me, I can't remember exactly what you said, you lost me. I felt put on the spot, I shut off, I withdrew consciously, suddenly, I don't know why.'

IAN: 'How did you do it?'

BOB: 'I withdrew, wanted to shut up, give up, I felt misunderstood. I probably misunderstood you, but felt very negative – I thought you were rude. I normally feel that everything within wants to reach out to people, but I went inside; you hurt me and I withdrew. I don't like that closed-up feeling at all. I have begun to open up through the love of other people. I want to understand where I went wrong.'

Bob is sitting with his arms crossed over his face, his fists clenched; he is in a curled-up position. The group shifts uneasily: some looked resigned to a tortuous analytical session.

BOB: 'I don't feel understood and I don't like my reaction; I don't like being like this, I want to restore

our relationship. I hate being distanced from
people, but it's not easy to open up to you.'

I take a plunge here. My hunch is that 'hurt' feelings cover
resentment about 'unfair' treatment. Bob backs off, rather
than owning his present resentment.

IAN: 'What do you resent about me?'

BOB: 'Oh, I need time to pray it through. I need to
         uncurl and relax like I was, I don't like being like
         this.'

IAN: 'Can you say that again, I'm not sure I under-
         stand.'

BOB: 'Yes. I want to say sorry for my reaction to you.
         I didn't want to resent you, but I did. I don't
         resent you; I believe that you were probably used
         by God to put a finger on something. I'm hurt, I
         withdrew. Someone else here said, "I often react
         like that in the group, I take things personally
         when they're not meant that way." '

IAN: 'You haven't answered my question.'

BOB: 'But really, I'm trying to understand what you
         sparked off inside me, I want to be open to God,
         I'm going slightly blank at the moment. I think I
         misunderstood where we were up to in the group.'

Bob continues by trying to explain in his own way events
of the group last evening. He is avoiding contact with me
by taking us to 'there and then', another place or time (last
night).

IAN: 'Please don't recapitulate last night, I suggest we
         remain in the here and now.'

BOB: 'You've brought it back into the present, I'm con-
         fused, I really don't think I'm trying to play
         games, I think we've got into a blind alley. I'm
         not sure if it's helpful.'

IAN: 'How do you blind yourself to what's going on?'

BOB: 'I was seeking to explain what happened last
         night.'

IAN: 'And so avoid the present moment. What *is* your
         blind alley?'

BOB: 'Oh, you ask me one thing, I give an answer, you

change the question, you take me off course. A blind alley is that I was trying to justify what I see, I was trying to explain it.'

IAN: 'How do you withdraw and go off course?'

We observe Bob folding his arms and fidgeting. The group is looking pensive, some people yawn. We are close to Bob's *impasse*.

BOB: 'It just happens, I don't do it consciously.'

He does not know how he frustrates himself and others, but *he goes on doing it!* He is frustrating me and the group now. I tell him this clearly and succinctly. Then I connect it with the hurt feeling coming through from last night. I need to clear this up.

IAN: 'Bob, I'm sorry if I was too abrasive and hurt you last night.'

BOB: 'I don't want anything to be between us.'

The atmosphere becomes easier. I make my first bid to change gear in the session. I want something more immediate than logic-chopping and reminiscing.

IAN: 'Would you like to lie down on the mattress?'

Bob curls up on the mattress and the group rests attentively, watching and waiting. Presently he begins his questioning routine again: 'Why? why? why?'

BOB: 'I felt very in touch with my feelings when physically curled up and then I lost touch through a line of questioning. I think I need to get back to those feelings and understand them. My most frequent prayer to God is "Why? What are you saying?" '

Bob never spoke a truer word: 'I lost touch through a line of questioning.' But he goes on doing it. 'Why' questions are a particularly good way of avoiding painful feelings or real contact with people. Answers always begin with 'because' and the process now becomes understanding, explanation, interpretation, analysis. This is well and good in its place, but in this context it becomes one more form of defensive 'games-playing'.

He curls up again.

BOB: 'Lord, why did I react that way? I get to "What are you saying?" *after* my "Why?" questions. I still want to keep saying things to the Lord at the moment. I want to tell him "Sorry" for the effect that I have on the group. Lord, it seems I talk too much. Lord, it seems I clam groups up, and I don't want to. Lord, I don't understand why, but I want you to deal with me.'

For God's sake, stop!

IAN: 'Stand up, Bob, look down at the mattress, play the role of God.'

I felt some impatience that even now Bob was playing his eternal record – the 'why' questions, the running commentary, the analysis. I intervene to cut this short by introducing a simple role-play. I ask Bob to stand at the foot of the mattress and literally to 'play God'. He and the whole group seem surprised at this audacity. He stands in silence for fully three minutes, (a welcome respite from the verbiage!).

BOB: 'Be still and know that I, the Lord, am God and not you. Seek my face and you will know.'

Bob returns to the mattress.

IAN: 'As you see his face, you'll perceive your own as a man who has boundaries. Sense your boundaries.'

At this point the time has come to change gear again to move out of the 'thought-mode' and into imagery. God's face will not be found, for Bob, in more questions and answers, but through pictures.

IAN: 'Picture a river and describe it to us.'

BOB: 'The river I see is bouldery and not too rushed as it flows. It's easy to watch, looks rather cold, it keeps very clean. I'm content just to watch it. I'd also like to tell somebody about it; no one especially, it's just that if I see something I enjoy I like to tell someone. In that instance it could be the first person probably that I knew. It could be a stranger.'

IAN: 'Become the river. As that river, talk to Bob about yourself.'

Another imaginative leap for Bob. At first he resists it. His reply is tentative.

BOB: 'I'll try.'

IAN: 'No, "try" means "fail". I suggest you *do it*.'

I explain what I mean by holding a dialogue with the river – Bob will play both parts.

BOB: 'It's not that I don't fancy it, I can't think of any-
           thing appropriate a river would say. Here goes
           anyway.'

Bob plays.

RIVER: 'Why are you looking at me?'

BOB: 'I find you restful.'

RIVER: 'But I'm always on the move.'

BOB: 'You can keep on the move and still be restful.'

RIVER: 'Perhaps you worry too much about things to do;
           let it all happen like I do. My flow never ceases,
           until someone dams me. Even if people try to dam
           me I just flow over the top. But I know you
           weren't thinking of damming me anyway.'

Ian intervenes. (I sensed that the river *had* been dammed and was avoiding saying so!)

IAN: 'But you *did* Bob, didn't you?'

BOB: 'I'm wondering why I ever thought about building
           a dam. I don't want any dams, it's an idea I've
           rejected; I just want to flow.'

IAN: 'Picture the river now as dammed.'

BOB: 'I'm finding difficulty because you're starting to
           talk about the river as me. I thought of damming
           the river and rejected it, I don't want to confuse
           you.'

RIVER: 'Why do people keep stopping me flowing?'

IAN: '*See the river as dammed.*'

I feel I am seeing an important clue to Bob's process. However, he refuses to cooperate. The *dam* is probably too painful an experience in his early life to contemplate for long.

The dam buster

BOB: 'It bursts with sudden force, it's triumphed, it's getting back to how it was before, uninterfered with.'

IAN: 'Picture the bursting.'

BOB: 'I can see it coming, beginning to break and then all coming, not sideways – just forwards. There's the tiniest trace of the dam left, just at the edges. It's as if it had never been there. The river is left totally unaffected. There's a little stick caught at the side bit by the dam. I feel sorry for the stick, I feel responsible for it.'

IAN: 'Become the stick.'

I cling on gamely to the last vestige of the cause of the problem!

STICK: 'I'm stuck because of someone who built that dam. Perhaps he's seen me and wanted to put me back in flow. It's so easy, it's great to be back in flow again. Perhaps he's all right after all because he's put right what he did wrong, he didn't mean to do it. I just like the flow. Bob, on the edge, built the dam.'

BOB: 'It was a silly idea to try and dam the river. It was fun, but I know what I already knew about the river – that it would break the dam in due course. I've just proved something to myself – the river's character is constant, always flowing, fresh, constant, beautiful, even if I do try and stop it for a while. But if I do mess around with natural flow there's a risk someone will get hurt, so perhaps I won't build a dam again. I don't want to interfere with the river, I just want to enjoy it. I still want to tell somebody about it because I've learnt something more about it. I'll tell Liz.

I just sat by the river and enjoyed watching it flow. I saw how fresh it was, and then I just started messing around and building a dam to see the effect on the flow. But, it burst very quickly. It

was odd watching the twigs get caught, but the
river's like it always was, and it's a lovely picture
of how the Lord works. It refreshes me. I want
to look at it. It's good to spend the time just
looking.'

IAN: 'Do you have a·sense of closure?'

BOB: 'Yes.'

IAN: 'It's a lovely picture of how you are created to
work, Bob. There is a flow within you. But a
river needs boundaries – it has banks which are
sometimes constricted artificially, to increase the
force and power of the water. When you dam a
river you need a containment area, otherwise it
will flood. People and situations don't want to be
flooded. Hitherto you have not been aware of your
personal boundaries; now they are your responsibility. The message of the picture is, "I'm going
to stop damming myself. If, however, I continue
to do it the results will be the same, whatever
the circumstances are, or whoever I find myself
with." '

IAN: 'How are you feeling now, Bob?'

BOB: 'I'm feeling more relaxed, more reinforced in my
desire not to get in God's way, but I'm aware that
I do. There's lots of working through required.
Why *do* I theorise? What is it that I'm actually
trying to cover over? It's something that always
seems to happen and doesn't help.'

With that dawning awareness in Bob that his theorising,
questioning and rationalising were in fact acting as a kind of
dam across his life, we closed the session in prayer. I prayed
against confusion which was discernible in his life. I prayed
for his powers of reasoning and thought to take their proper
place in the balance of his personality and not to dominate.
I prayed particularly for his wife, present in the group, that
together they would work at the new task of finding and
defining the boundaries, 'Lord, help them to strengthen the
river banks and to keep the flow powerful and clean.' Our
prayers may arise directly from the content of the work –

praying out the futile, time-wasting habits, and praying in the healing good news that our hearts need to hear.

Here are my own impressions of working with Bob – the man with no boundaries.

Firstly, some conflict puts us on our toes and alerts us to the need for something to be sorted out between group members now. I annoyed and irritated Bob by refusing to take his questions and theories at their face value; accusing him of games-playing and avoidance. The risk I took was that he would not follow my meaning and disappear in a huff. However, his own will to win and to move on through his difficulties was strong enough to keep him engaged with me. My covert message to Bob was, 'I do not intend to be confused, pushed around or thrown off course by your verbal bombardment. I will not collude with this game. The time is short and valuable. Let's get down to business.'

Bob is a man with an enormous desire to please; in his own words, 'everything within wants to reach out to people'. The hidden effect on others of this 'need-to-be-needed' is to produce a kind of resistance. It is as if we have to 'tune him out' to survive. This result is the opposite of what is intended. The flood of words may sound fine, full of sensible explanation or compassion, but the net result is to drown the victims, or using Bob's own picture, to dam the flow within *them*.

One turning-point in Bob's work was when we cleared up the atmosphere of tension and hidden resentment between us, (him and me). Another was when I asked him to play God and answer his own question. I believe the answers or solutions to our own problems lie within us, sometimes obscured or buried by the nature of the problem itself. In Bob's case, God asks him to be still and simply become aware of *his* sovereignty. The Lord says in effect, '*I* am God, and not you. Much of what you fuss and fret about can safely be left to me.'

In seeking God's face, Bob will know the all-providing and all-protecting nature of his Heavenly Father and will sense his own limitations and boundaries. He will become more keenly aware of his own identity. This in turn will enable him to co-operate with God's purposes in a more relaxed and flowing manner. This was perhaps the high point and meaning of the work.

I asked Bob to lie down on the mattress in order that his head might be lowered to the same level as the rest of himself and not in its usual dominant position. I asked him to visualise the river so that he would leave his usual thinking, questioning, rational style, and move into the strong language of picture and symbol.

The work did not provide any sudden breakthroughs or changes in direction, but it clarified and opened the door to the possibility of further growth-work by Bob. His picture of the river 'bursting the dam with sudden force' was a hopeful one. 'It's getting back to how it was before, *uninterfered* with.' Significant words indeed.

All parts of the visual imagery had significance. They represented parts of Bob, and I was particularly interested in the reply made by the stick: 'I'm stuck because of someone who built that dam.' I believe that stick represented Bob's perceptive faculty, his eyes and ears. Because of *someone*, sometime in the past, his ability to understand, his ability to use his eyes to see and his ears to hear had got stuck. The faculty of 'perceiving' had become atrophied in him. Not surprisingly, God asks Bob to be still and listen, and Bob, speaking of the river he's been looking at declares, 'It's a lovely picture of how the Lord works. It refreshes me, I want to look at it, it's good to spend the time just looking.'

Hopefully the next stage in Bob's healing will include the discovery of *who it was* who 'stuck' him at that particular point, who was responsible for damming the river and confusing his perceptions so badly. There will need to be some straightening out in *that* relationship and some prayers for healing of ears and eyes. Bob will then no longer need to play 'stupid' or 'confused' or 'weak', he can walk tall and realise his birthright as a member of Christ and an inheritor of the kingdom of heaven.

FOR COUNSELLORS AND THERAPISTS: METHOD-LEARNING FROM BOB'S WORK

Defences

Bob's defence was his *mind*. He wanted to take us on a conducted tour of its labyrinth ... a *head trip*! Normally respect defences. We all have a right to them and need them. In this case, however, sharp and persistent *conflict* was necessary to save me and the group from 'drowning'. Respect does not imply collusion. We may point out and bring to awareness 'games-people-play' but we should not 'force' or 'bully'. Progress is made, defences lowered by personal choice only. Sometimes an apology on the facilitator's part is both necessary and life-enhancing! Avoid those 'why' questions. They are hooks ... dangerous!

Acting-out

Do not hesitate to ask the working person to role-play. It might be himself at an earlier age, or a single aspect of her personality (Top-Dog, Under-Dog, Parent, Adult, Child). It might be the Tempter, or even part of the person's own body. Dreams provide a fruitful field of imagery and 'people' for role-playing too.

Fantasy

The imagery of the river provides a telling metaphor of Bob's own process. It illustrates vividly what effect he has on others (flooding, damming). The fantasy journey has its own hidden wisdom waiting to be revealed. Go with it, flow with it. It is waiting to reward you.

The Object of the Exercise

What are we attempting to do when we encourage Bob and the others 'to work'? By paying attention to every aspect of his presence in the group we highlight a *process*. This is 'what-he-does' in life, it is the way he chooses to 'come-across'. To the extent that it is unsatisfactory or frustrating we show it up for what it is. Awareness of my process makes the possibility of change and growth real. New options are presented. The working person makes a choice. The group's love and prayer can then confirm the start of a new way of being himself.

We should not go further with a person than they feel ready to travel. A sense of 'closure' in the group tells you when to stop.

BRINGING IT HOME

1. What effect do I have on a group of people? If it is other than what I really want, what causes this – how do I do it? Do I play games, subtle or unsubtle to keep them at arm's length, to dominate, or to control? (Perhaps your family will tell you – or a group you meet regularly with.)
2. Am I someone who needs-to-be-needed in such a way that others might feel threatened instead of helped? If you are in a trusting group you might risk asking each other this question!
3. In what ways do I expect to see and hear from God? (Cf.1 John 1:1)

SCRIPTURE

Joel 2:28–9 (NIV)
'And afterwards, I will pour out my Spirit on all people. Your sons and daughters will prophesy, your old men shall dream dreams, your young men shall see visions. Even on my servants, both men and women, I will pour out my Spirit in those days.'

Luke 17:20–1 (RSV)
Being asked by the Pharisees when the kingdom of God was coming, Jesus answered them, 'The kingdom of God is not coming with signs to be observed; nor will they say, "Lo here

it is" or "There" for behold, the kingdom of God is in the midst of you.'

PRAYER

O Lord, open my eyes that I may see, open my ears that I may hear the wonderful things of your Word, your meaning for me and the world in which I live. Amen.

FURTHER READING

Games People Play by Eric Berne (Penguin 1970).
Awareness by John O. Stevens (Real People Press, Box F, Moab, Utah 84532), pp. 137–67 on Fantasy Journeys.
Listening to God by Joyce Huggett (Hodder 1986).

Chapter Five

JOHN'S STORY: THE MICHELIN MAN OR WHO'S FOOLING WHO?

THIS IS THE STORY of the boy-next-door: the local lad who makes good by a mixture of bluff, good humour and ability. John reminded me of the 'shrewd manager' of Luke 16. That story provides a challenge for every preacher with its enigmatic tailpiece, '*I tell you, use worldly wealth to gain friends for yourselves, so that when it is gone, you will be welcomed into eternal dwellings*' (verse 9 NIV). Was Jesus teasing – a tongue-in-cheek story? Does it mean 'manage as best you can with the methods you know because ultimately it will all be stripped away'? Worldly cleverness, having-our-wits-about-us, are recipes for getting by and even succeeding in the rat-race. But where does the rat-race end and the eternal-dwellings begin? In this episode we follow John up to and over this threshold.

John was the third child born to a working-class family on a council estate. He was a clever boy who made his way in the world by intelligence and native wit. He was born to be a survivor, a winner by nature. Along with his real intelligence he had a well developed sense of 'one-up-manship' and could bluff his way through most of life's situations.

The main insight of his work is that when we choose to submit to God we have to stop phoney behaviour.

I took an immediate liking to John when I met him across

the meal table. Through the small change and preliminaries of conversation he and I were sizing each other up in the way men do, covertly assessing each other's power, status, background, weighing up whether this fellow is likely to prove useful to me, a threat to me, an ally or an enemy, and so on.

I perceived John to be a man of formidable intelligence and a bright, lively wit, an accomplished raconteur, someone with whom there would never be a dull moment. I could feel him shredding and analysing my offerings and replies in conversation and yet for all this I liked him. I felt, 'his heart's in the right place.' He let it be known that an accountant of his calibre was worth £300 a day anywhere he went to work. He came across as ambitious, wanting to impress and yet at the same time struggling, fighting and not entirely comfortable in his surroundings.

I found the 'work' that John did on the following day a profoundly moving experience. John soon recognised his endless capacity for bluffing and games-playing and other 'phoney' behaviour and submitted very willingly to a suggestion that he be rested in the Spirit. When this happens in ministry the Spirit of God comes powerfully upon a person, often causing them to fall over from a standing position. This was a method of working which I deliberately offered to John in order to help him move away from his 'head trip' (relying on intellectual superiority and analysis), and to confront the living God, warmly present within himself and ready to show him the way through his difficulty. When we rest in the Spirit we surrender to God the responsibility for and the control of our own 'process'.

It says a lot for John's faith and the faith of the group that this happened so effectively in the following episode.

When I use this method it is always with a careful explanation to the whole group so that they feel in a comfortable and co-operative state and are free to give their full prayerful attention to what is happening and to what God is saying and doing. The person to be so 'rested' stands at one end of a mattress on the floor and responds to the three baptismal questions (Do you turn to Christ? Do you repent of your

sins? Do you renounce evil?). He then feels confident enough
in God to allow himself to fall backwards as the Spirit releases
him. The experience has never to my knowledge harmed
anyone and people describe it as 'like falling into the arms
of a loving father, like having no responsibility even to stand
up, like floating back with the lightness of a feather and yet
retaining an awareness of the room and the people in it; a
deeply restful and refreshing experience.'

I would normally position a couple of group members to
be alongside the mattress to catch the person as they fall and
gently lower them to the pillow.

Even in this situation of intimacy with God, John finds
himself not entirely free from 'games-play'. He likes to anticipate your next move, like a conversational chess player, and
has to be gently chided about this. Notice in the work how
the real polarities of strength and weakness begin to emerge
from within him. The realities can emerge without fear. The
'work' begins to merge with ministry towards the end as I
pray deliverance for him and give a prophetic word and a
touch of healing from the Lord.

The big phoney

IAN: 'John, how would you like to use your time?'
JOHN: 'I find it's difficult to know. I'm aware it's right
         to work, can I begin with something that struck
         me yesterday? You said, "Anyone playing games,
         you would spot them." My initial reaction was
         fear because you could catch me out. I didn't want
         to be caught out, but I do need to go into things
         that underlie that fear. Can you help me to track
         down the games I play?'
IAN: 'Start by saying, "When I play my usual, familiar
         games . . ." and complete the sentence.'
JOHN: 'If I play my familiar games I would listen to you
         and look for the things that trigger a response in
         me and quickly sum up, evaluate and judge. I
         would offer you a critique of your approach so
         far, but I'm deliberately choosing not to do that.

If it was a games-play I would play a clever role or drop in something to get your response.'

IAN: 'And it would be phoney because you're only doing it to get a response and to start some kind of scenario resembling a verbal dual. Would you like to say how you play phoney?'

JOHN: 'This is how I am a big phoney sometimes. By knowing sufficient to be unchallengeable, except in situations where people are very sure of themselves.'

IAN: 'Are there many situations where you know sufficiently more to get away with it?'

JOHN: 'Oh yes. Either I know more or I'm better at expressing it.'

IAN: 'Talk to the group. Say, "I need to give the impression that I sometimes know more than I actually do and this is one of my games." '

John repeats this to the group and asks for their come-back. Seven people who by now know John quite well respond to him as follows:

1.   'I feel you're a big phoney.'

2.   'I want to know the real you, don't give me what you're not.'

3.   'Yes, you do try to impress and you can appear too good to be true.'

4.   'I'm aware of it, but when you do it I protect you because I know you're vulnerable.'

5.   'Sometimes I find you unsettle me and only realise afterwards what you've been doing. So it unsettles our relationship and it doesn't help.'

6.   'One word for you – bullshit. I'm bad at spotting games, I see them afterwards. I do sometimes wonder if you're being real.'

7.   'I'm a bit dense at spotting, I like to take you at face value.'

The group's response powerfully confirms John's suspicion that he has been rumbled. He seems very relieved now that all this is out in the open. His expression says, 'Good, now we can get on with it. How do I tackle it?'

There is an air of excitement and anticipation in the group as if important things which needed saying are out in the open. But John takes us on a further diversion before we are allowed to 'get on with it'. He protests that even if he wants to change it would be unsafe to do it 'too quickly'. I ask him how long he needs, a week, a month, a year – the rest of his life? There is talk about how much he has already changed – in the recent past. The group's energy and excitement are visibly waning.

The change John claims is a diminishing need to be 'in control'. I pick up this thread quickly. I have in mind to offer him a way of relinquishing control more effectively in the here and now.

Taking the plunge

IAN: 'How far do you want to pursue "to be able to not be in control"?'

JOHN: 'As far as I will go. I feel too "in control". I shouldn't be.'

IAN: 'I want you to relinquish control.'

JOHN: 'I don't know how to.'

IAN: 'Take off your glasses and shoes and stand at the end of the mattress and allow the Holy Spirit to take over. I suggest you abandon yourself completely to God.'

I explain to him and the group the procedure for resting in the Spirit. Then on an impulse I add:

'I have this phrase "blind man's bluff" in my mind, perhaps it illustrates something that's happening.'

Turning to John, waiting a little apprehensively, I ask,

'John, do you accept Jesus Christ as Lord and Saviour?'

JOHN: 'I do.'

IAN: 'Do you renounce all games-play?'

JOHN: 'I do.'

IAN: 'Do you repent of your sins?'

JOHN: 'I do.'

IAN: 'Do you wish to rest in the Spirit?'

JOHN: 'Yes I do.'

John sways once or twice and then falls backwards, caught in the arms of two helpers from the group. As soon as his head touches the pillow it is obvious that something is happening. His eyes are closed, but we are aware of rapid eye movements. It is as if he is watching an exciting film with physical responses to the events. His head is moving, his body is restless. After several minutes I question him.

IAN: 'What's happening, John?'

(His hand moves across his face.)

         'What is your hand doing?'

JOHN: 'My hand is trying to control my mind.'

IAN: 'You don't have to stop sensations, give yourself permission to go with the flow. What's happening now? I want you to be in touch with me. Where are you now?'

JOHN: 'My reasoning has returned, but slowly. My feet are cold, I would like something over them. I feel peacefully excited. I feel my arms are not what the rest of my body is. If God has slowed up my thinking process now I'm going to have to put up with it for a long time. My arms haven't been affected.'

IAN: 'Stay with the experience in your body and arms.'

JOHN: 'I feel I have no ability to move except in my arms. Into my mind comes the story of the paralysed man, let down before Jesus. Do I need to know his forgiveness and approval before I can walk?'

IAN: 'Do you want to talk to him about it?'

JOHN: 'But I haven't yet been taken in front of him. I'm not aware of him.'

IAN: 'Do you want to be taken in front of him?'

JOHN: 'I want my Dad.'

IAN: 'Let him come.'

JOHN: 'But he's with Jesus.'

IAN: 'What do you want to say to him?'

JOHN: 'I just want to feel safe. Dad, I never told you

anything, somehow you knew. I don't know whether I told you I loved you before you died.'

The sadness on John's face changes into a quality of rapt attention.

IAN: 'What's happening now?'

JOHN: 'I'm aware of Jesus, he's come to me and he's asking, "Do you love me?" If I say yes, he will say, "Feed my sheep" and I will say, "I cannot walk." '

IAN: 'Hear his question – don't anticipate dialogue, don't play games with Jesus.'

JOHN: 'Lord, I can say I love you and mean it, but I don't know what I should feel.'

IAN: 'Tell him what you do feel, not what you should feel.'

JOHN: 'I just feel empty, there's a hole in the middle of my chest.'

John is seeing and feeling his own weakness and inadequacy in the pictures of the paralysed legs (can't walk) and the 'hole' or missing bit where the heart should be. In the presence of Jesus we are often acutely aware of our own spiritual state.

IAN: 'Can you put your hand on the hole? What is your request to the Lord?'

JOHN: 'I wasn't designed to have a hole, I want to have it filled.'

The great exchange

IAN: 'We are with you in that prayer and we want to strengthen you now. Lord, will you fill the hole where love wants to come in. Come, Lord Jesus, more and more fill him with love, joy, peace. Come upon him, Lord. We ask that you will direct his mind.'

JOHN: 'Stop me rationalising about what was just asked.'

IAN: 'Fix your mind on the sovereignty of the Lord and tell him what is in your mind. You know what is stored up there.'

JOHN:	'Lord, is it wrong to want to help other people to understand what you are doing for people, for me?'
IAN:	'Listen to what he tells you about your mind. What does he say?'
JOHN:	'He's offered me *his* mind, it's an expensive trade, because he said, "With my mind see. There are feet to be washed, blind to receive sight, those without understanding to be taught" – but I'm not Jesus, I don't understand how his mind and my weakness can work together.'
IAN:	'So what are you saying to that amazing offer?'
JOHN:	'I accept your offer. I would like to ask you for some more things. If I see things the way you see them, well, you're going to need to be able to have control over my body, my tongue, my legs.'
IAN:	'So what are you asking for?'
JOHN:	'I need your body too.'
IAN:	'The mind of Christ and the body of Christ. Picture your body being permeated by his Spirit from head to foot. It becomes a temple, a home for the Spirit of God. You are still responsible for the body and the mind God has given you, but *his* ownership is being renewed.'

Once John stops programming the conversation this extraordinary confrontation can occur orchestrated by the Spirit. There is a long pause whilst its implications are realised.

Your strength . . . in my weakness?

JOHN:	(speaking to his body in a small childish voice) 'It's not fair, you're going to be afraid when you walk out. He'll take you places you don't want to go. Your new mouth will embarrass you, the family won't like it and you'll fail.'
IAN:	'Do you recognise that voice?'
JOHN:	'It's not me, because I say I'll always succeed.'
IAN:	'Then whose is the voice that says you'll fail?'
JOHN:	'It's my child.'

IAN: 'What do you want to say to your child?'

JOHN: ' "You failed because nobody helped you, but
        when you grew up and found someone to help
        you, you began to succeed." My child is so con-
        fused – holds two things in balance and believes
        them both. On the one hand I'm always outside,
        I have no friends; on the other hand I do, there
        are friends that as an adult I could walk up to,
        pick up with, as if I had seen them only yesterday.
        When we lived on the estate I was never accepted
        by the kids, I was never part of the group and I
        had to learn to cope with that. I had to cope with
        their parents who said that I was too stuck-up to
        go to the school their kids went to. But I learnt
        how to manage with the kids that went to the
        other school. I learnt how to control them and
        manipulate them. To control and manipulate –
        that's been part of my life.'

John, the 'shrewd manager', is describing how he has
protected and provided for the hurting child within himself
by controlling the outside world. I wonder if he is prepared
to relinquish these tactics for a different approach.

IAN: 'So John, what are you in this world for?'

JOHN: 'Which answer do you want?'

IAN: 'Choose the true one.'

JOHN: 'You mean the evangelical, Christian one? Because
        God chose to put me here.'

IAN: 'So the response of your life is what?'

I am indirectly challenging him to look at a choice of costly
discipleship. The risk of this question is that it might be too
far ahead of where John actually is. John, realising the import
of my questions, puts up a smoke-screen.

After a minute or two John says:

        'I'm choosing not to think or feel or whatever to
        respond to that.'

IAN: 'God put me here for no response?'

JOHN: 'God put me here to be part of what he created,
        but I'm fighting against something. My mind has
        stopped trying to find it.'

IAN: 'What is it?'

JOHN: 'To walk with him. I don't know whether that's
            from my mind or what. It's as if something is
            closing in on me and preventing me from taking
            hold of those words that will move me.'

IAN: 'Describe the thing closing in.'

JOHN: 'It's as if I'm on the inside of a box in my skull,
            but I'm outside observing it too. I'm inside and
            feeling it wanting to close me in.'

Deliverance

Something is attempting to close John's mind to the call. I
sense the presence of a powerful negative force and move
swiftly to counteract it.

IAN: 'John, hear the Word of the Lord. God did not
            give us a spirit of fear, but of power and of love
            and a sound mind. I bind that spirit of fear and I
            tell it to depart in Jesus' name. Leave him! Lord,
            please open the box, make it accessible to John,
            your chosen one. Let him know his identity, who
            he is and your purpose for him. Amen.
            What's happening, John?'

JOHN: 'The box no longer exists. Like orange segments
            it all fell back and within the box there is a shining
            object whose light fills my mind. A light to lighten
            the Gentiles. Now I have a picture of water flow-
            ing out of a hole in a cliff side, cascading down,
            white and powerful. And now a volcano bursting
            with fire and lava running down changing the
            shape of the volcano.'

Ian speaks a prophetic word.

            'You can have no other God but me, because I am
            a jealous God. You cannot set your ambition
            before your love of me.'

JOHN: 'I'm not afraid of you, but I am afraid of them –
            all those people. I don't know how to love them,
            but I know how to do things. I need to come to

terms with that. I can do different with your mind. My right eye is hurting.'

Ian prays:

'Lord, we ask you to touch and heal his right eye with the healing you want to give. Help him now to see with your eyes and think with your mind.'

JOHN: 'I'm afraid if I accept the whole deal and blow it, everyone knows about it. Can I cope with you all and the response?'

IAN: 'It's the body of Christ all around you. Pick yourself up.'

John stands on the mattress and looks round at the group with his arms spread out. He is undefended. He says:

'I have nothing to give you but what I am. I cannot be another person and I choose not to be another person.'

The group gathers round John to pray for him. Someone quotes 1 Corinthians 2:16: *'For who has known the mind of the Lord so as to instruct him? But we have the mind of Christ'* (RSV).

In conclusion, here are my own reactions and the learnings acquired during this session.

Reflecting on the phrase 'blind man's bluff' which occurred to me during the work, I imagined somebody coming blindfold into a circle of people who have all moved around. There is an element of calculated risk as you put the cushion down on an unknown pair of knees. Perhaps this says something about the calculated risk of resting in the Spirit, throwing yourself upon God and waiting to see what he will say, what he will show you. There is no way of pre-arranging the dialogue or defending yourself with games-playing. I am often amazed with the inner dialogues people have with the Lord himself, when I am prepared to take the risk of saying, 'listen to him'. I am never disappointed. The reply often has the quality of revelation.

Somebody I know well has a facial feature which is unusual, but in no way disfiguring. He, however, felt an enormous revulsion against his own appearance. How characteristic it was of the Lord to reveal himself, in a picture received by one of those praying for my friend, as the work-man at the carpenter's bench, sweating, working hard. As he turned to look up and greet my friend, stepping out into the sunshine, the Lord's face had exactly the same features as those which so bothered him. Understandably my friend said, 'That's going to take a lot of getting used to.'

God's strength is indeed made perfect in our weakness and again and again in the latter part of John's work the strength of Christ was meeting and permeating John's weaknesses as he acknowledged them. Our adversary does not give up without a struggle and I was aware of the backlash when I asked challenging questions like 'What are you in this world for?' John was aware of fighting against something and his mind blanking out. He then became conscious of the 'box' in his skull closing in and I became aware of spiritual conflict. I took authority in prayer to banish a spirit of fear, manipu-lation and control. John was then free to experience the light, the flowing water and the power of the volcano – all powerful biblical images conveying the presence of God himself.

The time available did not allow us to explore the meaning of the pain in the right eye, but I surmised that it was a significant touch on John's way of seeing himself and other people. Its message seemed to be 'blind man's bluff is over, I am about to see differently. The blind man's eyes are opening.'

John needed to repent of his former 'scripts' and the belief that he needed to control and manipulate people in order to survive. He began to do this when he said to Jesus, 'I can do different with your mind.'

The verses below from the Epistle to the Philippians would be a good, daily prescription for him as he renews his mind and establishes God's new way of looking and thinking within himself.

THE SELF—WINDOW

illustrates
John's Journey

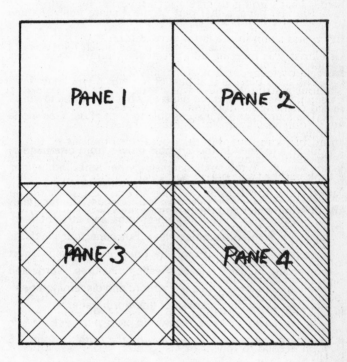

Pane 1: I know this part: you see and know it too.

Pane 2: I know this part, but I don't show you.

Pane 3: I don't know this part, but you may see it.

Pane 4: Neither of us knows what's in here. God knows.

JOHN'S JOURNEY – A METHOD-LEARNING BOX FOR MINISTERS AND COUNSELLORS

The Self-window
A helpful concept. The whole window represents 'myself'.

The first pane is that part of 'me' I share freely: I know it, you know it.

The second pane is that part of me which I know, but I don't tell you.

The third pane is that part of me which you know but I don't. I seem to be quite blind to what is obvious to you.

The fourth pane is inaccessible to both of us, 'God alone knows!'

John's journey in this chapter moves from one pane of the window to the next. Increasingly he *'walks in the light'* (1 John 1:7). As our John begins to speak truthfully about himself so pane two becomes less opaque. The facilitator and group give their true impressions and straight feedback: pane three becomes clear. But pane four yields its secrets only when Gifts of the Spirit are invoked. Direct prayer and ministry release 'Resting', Pictures, Words and Healing. Gifts of knowledge, wisdom and discerning-of-spirits clear away the darkness of the fourth pane.

'If we claim to have fellowship with him, yet walk in darkness, we lie and do not live by the truth' (1 John 1:6 NIV).

Spiritual Warfare
Moving into this dimension can be a life-changing experience. Fools rush in! Great sensitivity and much experience and training are called for. Everyone, however, must start somewhere and our Lord has promised the Spirit to lead us into all truth. 'Wholeness through Christ' – a movement for training in inner healing (see Glossary) – offers reliable training in using spiritual gifts and spiritual warfare.

> **Polarities**
> In the group so far we have encountered several pairs of opposites e.g. Fear/Confidence, Condemnation/Release, Anxious talking/Calm contemplation. In John we meet Strength/Weakness, Truth/Deception, Cleverness/Sincerity, The way of the world/The road of discipleship. *In working we are sharpening up the contrasts*, so that (a) an either/or choice can be made or (b) a satisfactory synthesis can be achieved.

BRINGING IT HOME

1. If someone in anger called me a 'big phoney' would there be some truth in the accusation?
2. How do I seek to create a good impression and ensure that others don't see through me?
3. Why do we sometimes 'embroider' the facts and sometimes tell only half the story?
4. What place does ambition play in my life?
5. How tightly am I holding on to my status, my plans and my hopes?
6. What would I give up for you, Lord, if you asked?
7. How do you interpret Paul's phrase '. . . *as deceivers and yet true*'? (2 Cor. 6:8).

SCRIPTURE

Philippians 2:1–11 (JB)

> *If our life in Christ means anything to you, if love can persuade at all, or the Spirit that we have in common, or any tenderness or sympathy, then be united in your convictions and united in your love, with a common purpose and a common mind. That is the one thing that would make me completely happy. There must be no competition among you, no conceit; but everybody is to be self-effacing. Always consider the other person to be better than yourself, so that nobody thinks of his own interests first,*

but everybody thinks of other people's interests instead. In your
minds you must be the same as Christ Jesus:

> *His state was divine,*
> *yet he did not cling*
> *to his equality with God*
> *but emptied himself*
> *to assume the condition of a slave,*
> *and became as men are;*
> *and being as all men are,*
> *he was humbler yet,*
> *even to accepting death,*
> *death on a cross.*
> *But God raised him high,*
> *and gave him the name*
> *which is above all other names*
> *so that all beings*
> *in the heavens, on earth and in the underworld*
> *should bend the knee at the name of Jesus*
> *and that every tongue should acclaim*
> *Jesus Christ as Lord,*
> *to the glory of God the Father.*

PRAYER

Lord, thank you for those experiences which deflate me,
bring me down to proper size. Forgive me when I get
puffed up with power, pride and self-importance. Let my
only ambition be to think with your mind and see with
your eyes. Let your strength and my weakness work
together. Amen.

FURTHER READING

The Gift of Inner Healing by Ruth Carter Stapleton (Hodder
1977). More about guided imagery in her concept of 'faith-
imagination'.

The Transformation of the Inner Man by John and Paula Sandford (Logos 1982), esp. Section 1 pp. 3–121 'Foundations'.
Spiritual Warfare by Michael Harper (Hodder 1983).

Chapter Six

LILLIAN'S STORY: THE GIRL WHO DIDN'T BELONG

HAVE YOU EVER said (or thought), 'I give up – nothing seems to work'? This person I'm trying to help has done it again. Hours and hours of counselling, pastoral chats, tender-loving-care, perhaps a genuine conversion experience – all seem to amount to nothing. The root of the problem has not been touched and all the symptoms have returned. The medical profession can help us with drugs to suppress the worst of these awful symptoms but there remains the unspoken challenge to the would-be healer to get to the bottom of it, to understand, relive, work through and find wholeness. The work which follows encounters the very beginnings of life: it is called primal-therapy.

Lillian is an unmarried girl of 27. Her face is small and birdlike. She wears jersey and jeans in a way which announces clearly she is of a younger generation than most of the group. Lillian has recently become a Christian, but it seems to have accentuated her feelings of rootlessness, lostness and a simmering, continuous hostility against society. She wants to come to terms with this.

In her 'work' she has a detailed recall of her origins and is able subsequently to verify these. Because this work concerns events preceding and immediately following her birth, we call it primal. Since her primal experiences she has gone on from strength to strength, gaining for herself a sense of identity, worth and purpose in life.

Lillian was born to a schoolgirl of twelve. She was adopted at four or five days by a farm worker and his wife and lived with her adoptive parents until she was seventeen. Her adolescent years were very disturbed and troublesome for her and for her parents.

Dr Bill Ellison and his wife Laura began to take an interest in her when she was referred to Bill suffering from anorexia nervosa. Lillian was at that time determined to leave home and after several attempts at establishing herself, accepted Bill and Laura's offer of a home with them.

She accepted Jesus Christ into her life as Lord and Saviour and it was as a very young Christian that she joined the small group who were able to help her reintegrate the traumatic events of her early life.

Bill and Laura continued to reparent Lillian for several years, subsequent to these events. There have been trials and tribulations, strains and stresses, but out of it all emerges a life taking shape and purpose from the Lord.

The group adopted her as a mascot, the baby of the group and yet wise for her years.

What follows is not a verbatim script, but her own account of the experience which lasted four hours, written at a later date.

Work along these lines was introduced into this country by Dr Frank Lake in the late fifties and early sixties. At first he used an LSD type drug to release the repressive barriers and obtain access to deeply stored memories of those events. Later on he discovered that people could find their own way back without medication in the company of a supportive and caring group of people. His discoveries met with great scepticism especially in the medical and psychiatric professions. However, much has been written, discussed and experienced since those days and many doctors, gynaecologists and midwives are now firmly convinced, as is the present writer, that no experience of our life, whether before or after birth, is beyond recall and I would add beyond the saving love of the Lord Jesus Christ.

When it was Lillian's turn to 'work', in spite of her apparent maturity and resolution, she displayed much of the anti-social aggression and rebellion which had accompanied her through teen-age years. She smoked, she ducked, she dodged, she played stupid, she played clever. In its turn the group displayed great patience, realising the cliff-edge she felt herself to be on.

Prematurely we tried resting her in the Spirit. It didn't work. (Lillian's resistance was too strong, the Spirit of God never forces himself into anyone's life.) Glossing over the length of time taken to begin, Lillian admits that it wasn't easy to hand over control of proceedings as she has a problem with authority!

Here is Lillian's account.

'I've received a lot of inner healing in the two years that I've been a Christian, but the most rewarding part of my healing has to be my 'primal', which took place when I had known the Lord for just a few months. What follows was to transform my whole being completely.

'I joined a group hoping for the primal experience, but not having any idea of what was going to happen. I knew very little of my birth as I had been adopted at five days old. I knew my mother was only about twelve when she gave birth, that she wanted to keep me, but it wasn't possible, and that she went back to grammar school after the birth.

'The primal work had been suggested by Christian friends as I had got many bad attitudes to life and people. I trusted that they knew what they were talking about when they said these things might stem from birth. I had learned in that short time that only good things come from God and that he in no way wanted to hurt us. Up until this time the Lord had shown me things in pictures and as the group started to pray I curled up. When I felt secure enough I 'let go' to the Lord and let him take charge. This meant allowing myself to flow with my own inner-process, which wasn't easy. I had a problem with authority, but then we all know who is the strongest in the end.

'The Lord would only show me what he wanted me to see and the first picture was of my father walking away from my mother. She didn't look very pregnant at this stage, but she did look very distressed. She stood up, stretched out her arms, begging him not to go. She then sat down and cried, not knowing what to do, it seemed. She looked lost, desperate and lonely. In the group I was myself crying now and asking why had he gone and left us? My mother then got up from the bench she was sitting on and went home.

'Next I saw her standing in a room in a house that was not familiar to me. Her stepmother was there (I knew she had one as Mom told me at some stage later in life) and her father. I can only gather that she was telling them she was pregnant. Then her stepmother started to hit her. I started to scream for someone to just get her out. We prayed and Jesus walked into the room and took her outside and cared for her.

'Further on in the pregnancy my mother walked into the same room and stood by her stepmother who was sitting at the table. My mother seemed to ask her if she could keep me when I was born. She began pleading with her. I thought she was about seven months pregnant at this time. An argument broke out and her stepmother got up from the table and slapped my mother around the face. Mother then flew upstairs and locked herself in her bedroom. In temper she banged her fists and head against the wall. Exhausted she lay down on her bed and looked down at the bulge in her stomach. It was as if from inside her I knew what she was thinking and I called out, 'No, Mom, don't do it.'

'I've no idea how long she stayed in her room, but I soon became hungry. Mother wasn't eating and therefore starving me. I found myself calling from inside her to "please eat" so that I could get nourishment.

'At this point we prayed again and the Lord gave me a lovely picture. He walked into the room with a plate of sandwiches. As he turned to leave the room he gently patted my mother's stomach.

'The next pictures were most helpful to us understanding a lot of my attitudes. Mother was now in hospital and was lying on a bed looking very frightened and as though she didn't know what was going to happen to her. I then had a picture of myself curled up inside the womb. I said out loud, "ouch", which we interpreted as mother being examined internally. There was no room to move now and I desperately wanted to stretch and get out. I shouted from inside, "push"; nothing happened, I felt completely trapped and stuck. Finally I began to give up, there was no energy left in me or mother. Then I stopped breathing. Mother was screaming. I was aware of something around me changing, probably the waters breaking. I was thinking I don't want to die, but can't do any more, there's no way out, I can't get out. I was in complete panic, my heart beating so fast, and then it began to slow down, then nothing.' (At this point in the work Lillian seemed to blank out. The medical people in the group wondered if it could be because mother had been delivered by Caesarean Section. This was in fact not the case, we learned later. She had been anaesthetised during the birth and we had the strong impression of a forceps delivery.)

In the working group, Lillian moves, pushes and appears to be aware of coming out. Her bodily movements correspond with those of a baby emerging from the birth canal. The account continues.

'Suddenly there was an enormous rush of air, filling my lungs and a feeling of someone pressing on my chest and of pipes in my throat. A doctor then picked me up and I looked down on my mother. I reached out a hand to her, but as I did the doctor began to walk away. I screamed out, "Don't take me away, I want my mother." As the distance between us became greater I screamed louder, "Don't take me away from her, she wants me." Then the door closed between us. I was never to see her again and for all I knew she was dead as she lay motionless on the bed. There was no warmth, no comfort or love, just coldness and hardness. I was put in a cot in a room alone, at least I felt alone, and there I cried for ages. There was no point to anything now. I should have given up completely, there was no point in living on.

'Then a nurse came and picked me up and thrust a bottle down my throat. I don't want this I thought, go away and leave me alone. I refused food for a while. I'll show them too many dry nappies and they'll get worried.

'We prayed again and Jesus came into the scene and gently lifted me up and fed me and carefully put me back into the cot.

'Next, another lady came into the room. She wasn't a nurse because she didn't have a uniform on. She picked me up and started to carry me out. I tried looking back for my mother, and I again began thinking, "Don't take me away". I wanted to know where she was, but it was no good. I did not cry this time. Already the hardness and protective walls were within me. I was taken in a car to a household which I decided I didn't like from the word go.

'There was yet another woman in this house and after a short while she told me she was my mother. She must have thought me stupid and she kept fussing around me. I didn't need that from her or from anyone else for that matter. I very much wished she would go away and leave me in peace. I had been put there and there I would have to stay. I didn't have any choice. Already people were controlling me and so they all continued to.

'I had by now, at hardly a week old, got an attitude that stayed with me for many years. Try as I would later I could not break the pattern. From it came words like "There's no way out; they've taken me away from her; it's a cold and hard world anyway; I'll have to protect myself, no one else will; don't fuss round me, I don't need you; yeah, yeah all right, I'll do it if that's what you want, but I'm all right, never mind just let me get on with it; go away, leave me alone." '

Lillian had stopped breathing briefly during her primal just before the birth sequence and in the following sequence she stops again, much to the alarm of the doctor in the group. The account continues.

'There was an incident when I was about two years of age. I must have been ill because Mom settled me down on the couch in front of the fire and then left the room. I then stopped breathing. There was complete panic. Then as suddenly as it had stopped it started. Soon after Mom walked into the room to check me. I'm all right I thought, with the attitude of "who cares anyway?"

'A short while on, I'm not sure of my age then, I see myself peering round a door looking at a man. I don't think I knew who he was because I went and asked Mom who he was. She took me by my hand and then put me on his lap. I immediately jumped off and went and hid at the bottom of the stairs. Mom came and told me not to be so silly, it was my dad. I never had a dad at the hospital, so why now?'

Lillian's account in its objectivity, and matter-of-fact retrospect, can give very little sense of the vivid and electric experience that the whole group shared in while she was reliving these episodes. It was as if some heavenly editor had selected episodes for an action replay and given us all the significant highlights we needed as in *Match of the Day*. The difference was of course that our human antennae, both emotional and spiritual, were fully and completely involved as the drama unfolded. It seems that some kind of human presence and receptivity is necessary before these deep places can be safely visited. I believe our prayers and faith enable the Lord to make himself present in healing and nurturing ways at critical points. These were points at which baby as well as mother would have felt rejection, desolation and panic. I believe too that allowing this process to be relived and healed in this way removes forever the sting and hurt left deep in Lillian's psyche. She will quite literally never be the same again.

The second part of her account is equally fascinating. It chronicles her attempts to get in touch with her natural mother which followed this work, and verifies many of the circumstances and situations which were revealed in the course of the work.

The account continues.

'There were various things after this that were continuous patterns of life. I was always curious about my real parents, but as my adoptive parents were told very little they were not able to tell me much. When I was eighteen I contacted the Social Services to try and find my mother, but they were unable to help, except, when last heard of, she was living in the Peterborough area. I didn't persist in the matter and let it go. I didn't really have a good reason for finding her anyway, I told myself. But now, after the primal experience, my curiosity was aroused even more. I wanted to find out how much was true and how much was my imagination or interpretation. Also I suppose, in my mind I had through the years cursed her because there was no one I looked like or was part of.

'So I went to the Social Services again: the law had changed. My adoptive Mom had assured me a few years before that if I ever wanted to find my natural mother it was okay by her. The officials were unable to help again and I felt they didn't want involvement or to even consider the matter. What they did suggest was that I went to the next building in the square to get an address from which to obtain my original birth certificate. Little did they know that that was the best help they could give me. I went in and told the man there I had been sent and asked for the address. He asked what hospital I had been born in. It was the local one, and he said that my certificate should be right there on his shelf. With that he took down a large book, I knew the surname of my mother and he opened it and there it was! "This can't be true," I thought, "perhaps the Lord *does* want me to find her." He wrote out a copy, I paid £4.00 for it, thanked him and bounced out into the courtyard. On the certificate was the address mother was living at when I was born. To my surprise it was in our local town. With great excitement I set off for that house in the knowledge that she did not live there any more, but hoping that I might find out something.

'The person living there told me to try next door as she had been there for many years. I knocked and asked her if she had known them, and she said, "Yes", she did vaguely remember them and "Oh, I think they had, I think the daughter had a baby." Funny she should remember that bit I thought. "Yes, me", I said and that made her mouth drop. Poor woman, perhaps I ought not to have said it. Anyway, she said that mother's father was the editor of the local newspaper, why not try the office in town, and also that he was the local Methodist preacher! This was news to me.

'I set off for the press office, moving through the streets so fast my feet hardly touched the ground. When I got there the office was closed. I had forgotten it was half day and was disappointed. Also I was almost forgetting the Lord. I had only known him three months at this time and had only a small amount of faith in anything other than inner healing. But I can remember standing in the middle of the small precinct praying under my breath, "Lord, if this is your will that I should find my natural mother, then please continue to guide me in the right paths or else shut the doors." This was a new way for me in trusting the Lord.

'Next day I managed to contact the present editor who told me that his predecessor had moved to the Lanchester Times and that was all he knew. I got home, rang directory enquiries and got the number of the newspaper office there. A girl answered and said that the gentleman in question had retired, she even obliged with his address and telephone number as well. I hung up, and then sat back to have a careful think – if he is retired he would be getting on in age and I had no idea of his state of health and in no way did I want to hurt or upset anyone. Also, there was the fact that I *should* be doing this through Social Services. I decided that if I got through to the old man then I would say that I was an old school friend and was wanting to contact her again. A lie I knew, so prayed before ringing. I confirmed who he was and then said my bit. He didn't sound too convinced, but did not hesitate to give me my mother's number. I thanked him and hung up as quickly as possible.

'Here in my hand I had my mother's telephone number, I couldn't believe it! What was I to do with it? No way could I ring her up just like that, who knows what she was like – she might be happily married and have never mentioned me and may even have forgotten the past. Although in the back of my mind were the words that my adopted mother had often said, "Your real mummy wanted to keep you, but . . ." I went to one of my Christian friends and told her. She asked if I would like her to ring for me. I didn't know what to do. I knew I would not have got this far without the Lord's help and I trusted him to know what he was doing. It was agreed that my friend would ring. As she dialled the number and started to explain, I held my breath. Before she had finished speaking, a voice at the other end almost screamed, "She's mine, she's mine, I have been looking for her since I was thirteen." That was certainly not what I expected her to say – I don't know what I expected really. I was not able to speak to her, but said that I would ring back. What did go through my mind, and what did bring me back to earth, was the fact that I wasn't hers, but the Lord's and certainly *didn't* want to go and be with her for good. So we prayed before I rang her back. Besides I had often thought to myself through the years that I was glad to have a good home and two parents. It would not have been right for her to have kept me, with her being so young.

'I rang her back. I can't say that I enjoyed the conversation really as she talked all about herself. I don't suppose she knew what to say, but looking back from eighteen months later and having matured a lot, I think she was right to tell me she did not agree with the way things had been and that she had not wanted me adopted, but that the authorities had taken charge. She was very bitter at 'them', but as far as I was concerned they had done what they thought to be the best thing. She was still fighting mad – one powerful woman.

'We decided to meet at my friend's house. The next day I rang my grandfather back to explain who I was, and to my surprise he said, "I thought that's who you were". He had guessed and asked me to go and see him as he was on his own. He said that my mother was not over friendly to him these days, but hoped that our meeting went all right. He said he would like to see me and from the way he said it, I believed that he really did. It was almost as if they expected me to arrive on the scene and they certainly had not forgotten that I existed.

'The Sunday that I was to meet mother I awoke quite early. I hadn't told my adoptive parents all that had happened and that I wanted to meet her, and I now felt I ought to. So I got into the car and drove over to see them. I arrived before they were up and so let myself in and made them a cup of tea. I went and sat on the bed and told them. My dad didn't make a sound and then said, "We don't want to lose you." I was astounded to hear him say that, it wasn't like him and I just said, "Don't worry, you're not going to."

'Mom later said that he kept on saying it all the week. It was just like that time when there were appeals during the adoption procedure. I hadn't been that close to them, I didn't realise that I meant so much to them. I've since learnt and accepted this.

'The doorbell rang and I became rigid on the spot. I heard voices in the hall, and quietly I peered round the corner and came face to face with her. It was almost like looking in a mirror, she was the same build as me, perhaps slightly smaller. How on earth she had a baby at twelve years old that weighed almost nine pounds I don't know. She wore the same glasses as me and we soon found out where a lot of my personality came from and it made me decide that I wanted the Lord to make me different. She had with her a friend who was quite weird, her oldest son who was half Arab by another father, another son by yet another father and at home two little girls by (you've guessed) another father. One thing I found out was that she had been adopted too and who knows what before that. But, praise the Lord, he was changing the pattern with me, although I must admit that I had started on the same downward path as her before I asked the Lord into my life.

'It's funny, I can hardly remember a thing she said. It was as though I saw her, but like she was speaking another language. Perhaps that was the way the Lord wanted it. It was the primal experience that I wanted to find out about. Had it happened like that or not? Mother told me she was beaten by her stepmother, she was in labour for quite a time and she was anaesthetised at the last minute and there was panic. She never saw me. The most remarkable thing was that she *did* shut herself in her bedroom during the pregnancy and didn't eat, but had at that time comforted herself by playing a record called "I walk with God".

'What of my father? Well, he was the son of grandfather's

second wife, so although there was no blood tie between him and mother, he was her stepbrother.

'I wrote to her a couple of times but stopped as there wasn't much sense in it at the time and she never wrote back and I dropped the whole thing. It seemed the right thing then. I didn't go and see granddad either, as I told myself I would.'

Lillian did in fact make that visit eighteen months later and also had a long telephone conversation with her natural mother subsequently.

Lillian took her belated 'A' Levels in sociology and psychology. (Her natural mother has a degree in sociology and teaches social workers.)

Someone may ask, 'What are the benefits of such probing, such reliving of the dim and distant past? Isn't it all better forgotten, hasn't it all gone down the river?' I believe the events and patterning of our beginnings have an effect which can last right through life, just as the patterning inside a cucumber is the same from one end to the other. I believe that significantly to alter that patterning we have to revisit the original scenes in the healing presence of the Holy Spirit. We can then be released from negative faith-judgements, attitudes and 'scripts' which have kept us in the bondage of resentment, rejection, hatred or fear for many decades.

For over a week after this 'work' Lillian was in a bad way emotionally. It was as if a depth charge had been dropped to bring up a wreck at sea. Bits and pieces of debris were surfacing for days afterwards. She confirms, however, that the experience took her back to a real acceptance of what had happened.

'These are my beginnings and now I have let them become really part of me. These are my people and I know them. Having met my natural mother I can now feel free to make an adult choice to belong, gladly and willingly, to my adoptive mother and father. My faith has been confirmed. Jesus really does what he promises – he has done it in me, in a way I could not have dreamed of or anticipated. My mother is like me, but I now wish to be *unlike* her in many ways. I have finished with resenting the Social Services for separating us;

I have finished with resenting my adoptive parents – I believe them when they say "We don't want to lose you." The links are strengthened. I can now believe what they've always told me, that my mother desperately wanted to keep me, but was unable to, and it was not her fault, I have no need to go on blaming her. I know that we wanted to reach out and touch each other, but that we were snatched away. I know too that my anorexia and all the attitudes associated with it started in the intensive care unit: "You can't give me what I really need, so I don't want your food or your care, I'll work it out on my own." The Lord has renewed my mind, I can forgive the people, I can forgive the events, I feel reconciled within to myself and my origins, the future can only get better, I am no longer bound by my past.'

When we have within us something unfinished, a crying need still there deep inside, an experience such as this teaches that inner healing is possible. When a life is committed to the Lordship of Jesus Christ it will begin as soon as we are willing to give him access. For Lillian, square one was the place to start.

THE ROOT OF THE MATTER –
A PRIMAL-LEARNING BOX
FOR THE PROFESSIONALS

Primal Therapy – Necessary?
The writings of Arthur Janov and the later writings of Frank Lake might give the impression that everyone needs to go through the 'primal hoop' in order to be saved! Not so – many births are normal, not in the least traumatic and all begins very well. Some *are* difficult involving perhaps Caesarian section, forceps or long spells of difficult labour. Nevertheless baby is resilient and struggles through relatively unharmed. But for others, the Lillians of this world, the events leading up to birth, birth itself and the events immediately following are so traumatic as to scar the personality for life, and to produce persistent behavioural prob-

lems. There is a crying need within which has to be met. There is an enormous scream waiting to be screamed-out.

Indications for primal therapy are:

1. Sufficient ego-strength and determination to leave no stone unturned on the part of the one working.

2. A loving prayerful group, unlikely to take fright, and having four hours to give, if necessary.

3. A facilitator who has familiarised himself or herself with this mode of working and preferably has completed his or her own primal-work.

4. A sense of being really led into deeper waters (everything else has given only temporary relief).

How to start

Sometimes a person will begin to feel a need to curl up and feel small quite spontaneously. They 'talk themselves into it'. Sometimes it is a natural consequence of resting in the Spirit. Sometimes a facilitator may ask you to lie down, curl up and – given your permission and willingness – talk you back into the womb. From then-on-out the process is yours! Deep and regular breathing keeps your process-energy moving along.

Keep in touch

As helping person, ensure that the working person is continuously in touch, responding to your questions or commands. If this link is in any danger of being broken call '*stop*' and with a sharp clap of your hands bring the person back to present awareness. The work is personal but must never be private. We can be 'down there' sweating it out with mother *and* aware of our personal helper simultaneously. Often the latter will invite us to stop – just in order to have a rest!

Prayerful re-birthing

As we encounter difficult or stuck places in the birth process so we are able to pray the Lord's presence and healing love right in. Fears, anguish or even revulsion, if present in the mother, will be reproduced in the baby. These 'contrary spirits' need to be dealt with appropriately. Very early 'scripts' (e.g. Lillian's 'There's no way out.' 'It's a cold, hard world.' 'I don't need you.') will appear and need to be gently and firmly altered. Even *baby's* 'decisions' can now be revoked and repented of. They then lose their grip on the adult's belief-system and life.

How to finish
It will be obvious to everyone present when the birth is complete. The adult has been working very hard indeed to be 're-born' and will often feel exhausted and fragile. Suitable 'mothering', rest and nourishment should be available. Definitely not the time to drive back to work or be expected to socialise!

BRINGING IT HOME

1. Are you aware of your beginnings?
2. How do you feel these days about new moves, or stepping out in faith? (There are often 'echoes' of primal experiences affecting us today.)
3. 'As it was in the beginning, is now and ever shall be.' True for God, need it be true for you and me?
4. Meditate on our Lord's time in the womb and his early mothering (Luke 2). If you have a prayer partner, pray for each other in this area.

SCRIPTURE

Jonah 2:1–9 (RSV) (An experience which has distinctly primal overtones.)

Then Jonah prayed to the Lord his God from the belly of the fish, saying, 'I called to the Lord, out of my distress, and he answered me; out of the belly of Sheol I cried, and thou didst hear my voice. For thou didst cast me into the deep, into the heart of the seas and the flood was round about me; all thy waves and thy billows passed over me. Then I said, "I am cast out from thy presence, how shall I again look upon thy holy temple?" The waters closed in over me, the deep was round about me, weeds were wrapped about my head at the roots of the mountains. I went down to the land whose bars closed upon me for ever; yet thou didst bring up my life from the Pit, O Lord my God. When my soul fainted within me I remembered the Lord; and my prayer came to thee, into thy holy temple. Those who pay regard to vain idols forsake their true loyalty. But I with the voice of thanksgiving will sacrifice to thee; what I have vowed I will pay. Deliverance belongs to the Lord.'

PRAYER

Lighten our darkness, Lord, we pray, and in your mercy defend us from all perils and dangers of this night. For the love of your only Son, our Saviour, Jesus Christ. Amen.

FURTHER READING

Tight Corners in Pastoral Counselling by Frank Lake (DLT 1981).
The Primal Scream by Arthur Janov (Abacus 1973).
The Feeling Child by Arthur Janov (Abacus 1977). Both Janov's books are academic but very readable – suitable for mental health professionals.

Chapter Seven

SAM'S STORY: THE MAN SITTING ON A VOLCANO

'PLEASE DON'T BE angry with me' is a phrase children use to cover the sort of misdemeanours which are bound to be found out. Don't be harsh: don't hurt me. 'Now don't you make me angry' is a phrase parents use to warn that there's danger ahead. On either side is a genuine abhorrence and fear of that wild, crazy emotion which makes us do and say things which we later regret. We learn to control it, we learn to conceal it – but it doesn't go away. Is there a way to handle our resentments and aggressive feelings constructively and positively? Sam's story reveals a decisive change in a short time. And he had so much to be angry about . . .

At the age of 26, and newly married, Sam had been involved in a serious car accident. It had left him paralysed from the waist down and confined to a wheelchair. He had been able to continue his job as a computer programmer after two very long spells in hospital. He is now thirty, and gives an impression of strength and determination to overcome his setbacks.

Somehow the early encounters between us had put him on his guard. He saw me as some kind of professional who would be unwilling to relate to him in a personal way. The importance of this perception can be seen as his work unfolds. The long delay and elaborate precautions that seem to be necessary before he is willing to work are in direct proportion to the strength of the emotion to be released. He is saying in effect, 'Before I let you know the volcanic feelings that are erupting in my heart, I want to know that I am safe with you.'

After the initial parley I adopt two role-plays to help Sam get on with it. I adopt the posture of the doctor, the professional, the one who seems quite unapproachable, and then later, kneeling at his wheelchair I adopt the role of Jesus, who will serve and help you once you are ready to work.

The episode needed a stick or encounter bat and a large pile of cushions and pillows. The method employed in reaching the angry feelings within Sam was 'acting-out'. The results were that things he knew before in his head became connected to the real, underlying situation in his heart.

We were all able to learn that anger is simply anger, and as such morally neutral. When hidden and denied it is a consuming fire within and leads to all kinds of ill health, of mind and body. When expressed it can be destructive and hurtful, it can result in war, hot or cold. When submitted to the Spirit of God, however, it can be converted to useful purposes.

In the group Sam seems alert and restless.

Uptight

IAN: 'How are you this morning, Sam?'

SAM: 'I feel less uptight than I was. It's difficult to see where this energy is coming from.'

IAN: 'Stay with your present awareness.'

SAM: 'Well, I'll start with yesterday when you were winding us all up. You were putting yourself in a part where you weren't relating to me as a person. You were playing a role, not someone I could touch. I suppose that whatever I say, you'll take as material for what you do. Whatever I say to you doesn't affect you.'

IAN: 'That's an assumption of enormous proportions.'

SAM: 'You give an appearance of invulnerability and untouchability; my request is to ask you to be vulnerable to me. Let me get through to you.'

IAN: 'How do you want to touch me?'

SAM: 'So that I have the possibility of hurting you, although that's not what I wish to do. So that I'm not just another member of another group. I might be able to start by telling you what I think of you now.'

IAN: 'Yes?'

SAM: 'I sense your enormous strength, you could hurt me physically and verbally, I tremble a bit at that.'

IAN: 'I feel a strange mixture of compassion and apprehension meeting you in a wheelchair.'

I notice that Sam's right leg has violent spasms, it seems to want to drum on the wheelchair.

IAN: 'What are you doing with your right leg and foot?'

SAM: 'Oh, it's quite involuntary.'

IAN: 'I need to pick up *any* signals that are being dropped into this group . . . I'll try and be more open and real to you, but I need to hold onto my role as leader. It's true, I may have forgotten your name in six months' time, but all my care and attention at this moment are for you. It's a limited love, however, and a limited commitment. I offer you 100 per cent attention between now and lunchtime.'

SAM: 'I accept that, but I don't like the idea of relationships that don't mean anything for a longer time.'

IAN: 'Is it unsettling for you?'

SAM: 'Yes, I'm wanting to know that I mean something to somebody. If I spend time and put myself into a relationship and they move off elsewhere, what was the point of it?'

Somebody special

IAN: 'Can you change that question into an "I-statement"?'

SAM: 'I want to be somebody special.'

IAN: 'Turn it over, try saying, "Sometimes I feel nobody special." '

SAM: 'No, it doesn't fit in terms of this relationship.'

IAN: 'Tell me about your specialness.'

SAM: 'I don't know that I matter really. I'm not sure really.'

IAN: 'Doesn't sound as if it were true. Tell me about how ordinary you are.'

SAM: 'I'm an ordinary guy, but I'm special to those who are special to me. If I'm wanting to open myself I want them to do the same to me. I want them not to abuse me for opening up, I want people to be straight with me.'

IAN: 'Can you say that to me?'

SAM: 'I want you to be straight with me. I don't want you to be gushing all over me, and then mean nothing to you when you're with someone else.'

IAN: 'How do you want to spend the time we have left, about an hour?'

I speak here with a slight impatience, aware of barriers still between us but unable to define them.

SAM: 'I don't want to keep you up on a pedestal, just to facilitate. I want to understand my reaction of turning myself off to you. I recognise it as something I do. I do it when people approach me professionally and not personally.'

The pompous doctor

My hunch is that he *does* want to keep me on a pedestal so that he can be really and justifiably angry with me. I deliberately exaggerate my 'position' of superiority and expertise.

IAN: 'I will set myself up professionally. Here I am a professional.'

(I strut pompously round the group, looking down on Sam.)

'I am running this show, I am the boss. I don't care a fig about dialectical materialism [this was a phrase Sam had used last night].'

SAM (joining in the charade with a kind of hopeless desperation):

'I just can't win with you. I can't play your game,
you'll just score points, every way you'll win.'

IAN: 'Yes, I'll win, I have the nuclear bomb behind my
back. I have the power to make you conform.
You can take it or leave it.'

SAM: 'Whatever way you win, I can't touch you.'

IAN: 'Yes, I'm Godlike.'

SAM: 'You're removed from me. Even if I come to a
change of heart, you win. If I defy you and stay
hostile, you win. I cannot touch you.'

The role-play rambles on, losing energy, becoming half-
hearted. We both realise uneasily that we are boring the
group.

After some exchanges across the room Sam swivels his
wheelchair sharply and moves out of the group, indicating
that he needs to visit the loo. The need for a break also
indicates that we are close to a trouble-spot! People are looking tense and worried now as if experiencing frustration.
Bob voices the group's feeling.

BOB: 'It seems like there's been a twenty-four hour
negotiation going on.'

The group discusses what has been happening in a desul-
tory way during Sam's absence. Suddenly someone makes a
connection between Sam's reaction to me and that to his
hospital doctors after the accident. The penny drops, light
dawns. When he returns I encourage him to speak directly
to them using cushions nearby to represent them. He begins
in a controlled voice.

SAM: 'You're *not* God. I really cannot *stand* the way you
talk about me rather than to me. My concept of a
person is wholly lost, I'm just a bunch of symptoms in a bed and no longer a person.'

Ian, noticing Sam's hands clenching into fist, says:

'Let your hands tell you what you feel.'

SAM: 'It's not fair for you to do this to me.'

IAN: 'How big do you feel when you say that?'

SAM: 'Really, really small. Depersonalised, utterly
powerless, on the bed. I need you to be operating
on me. I need you to help me, I'm in your power

and you're blinking well not worthy of it. You're just a guy who's happened to take medicine and learnt how to operate. You're just ordinary, no one special.'

IAN: 'Sam, will you re-enact things so that the power-less Sam can express his strength during that long process of "being done good to"?'

SAM: 'I'm back in the ward. The first time I was here for six months after the accident. Who's going to want me any more? I'm robbed of my manhood and my worth, it's not fair.'

Friend and brother

I cross the room to Sam's wheelchair and kneel beside him, sensing that this is the impasse. This is where Sam is going to need the support of someone alongside.

IAN: 'Sam, I'm here to serve you this weekend, to wash your feet, because he does that for us. I want to do whatever you need.'

SAM: 'Yes, I respond a lot more to that. I really warm to your kneeling and the second approach. I hardened to the first approach. I love the servant bit, I love you, I suppose.'

IAN: 'Your left hand, look, it's saying something, it's pushing around.'

SAM: 'It's the doctors. I hate doctors, I felt it when you said, "Godlike". Having spent a lot of time in hospital, I hate doctors.'

IAN: 'I can see that's true.'

SAM: 'They are messing me about and not caring.'

Sam addresses the cushions on the floor.

'I *hate* you because you assume Godlike power. You stand at the end of the bed and talk about me, I'm just a body in a bed, because there's no way I can touch you or get through to you, you're totally impersonal towards me.

Then there's that other six months in hospital. I felt shame and guilt, I shouldn't have gone back

in there. I felt the scorn of the doctors, they were
scorning me.'

IAN: 'Try being scornful of them.'

SAM: 'You pathetic idiots, you're not worthy to be in
this position. What gives you the right to be like
that?'

IAN: 'Do you overhear conversations at the foot of the
bed?'

SAM: 'Yes, consultant talking to junior doctors about
me. You don't care that I'm stuck in this ghastly
place, not being able to do anything I want to do
in this situation that I'm in. I resent this ghastly
place, I really hate hospital.'

IAN: 'It *sounds* as if you hate it.'

SAM: 'I absolutely loathe it. Aaaaagh.'

Sam shouts out his anguish and Ian encourages him to do
it again and again.

IAN: 'Stay with that and what your hands are doing.'

I pass him a towel to wring and he wrings it violently
between his hands.

SAM: 'I really loathe you, I hate you.'

Sam's face is contorted.

IAN: 'Your hands are saying a lot and your face, but
your voice is not matching. Get them together, let
your voice reflect what you are doing and feeling.'

SAM: 'I'm snarling between my teeth, I'm really going
to give it to you, you can't believe just how much
I hate you.'

The swine!

At this point I pile cushions and pillows near the chair and
give Sam the encounter bat to replace the towel.

IAN: 'This pile of cushions now represents the hospital,
the treatment and the doctors. Take your time,
get into your real feelings about them all. Then do
what you need to do. Move into your strength.'

Sam talks to the pile and belabours it with the encounter
bat.

SAM: 'So, *swine*, so, aaaaagh, aaaagh.'

Side-swiping at the pile, scattering pillows and cushions in all directions.

IAN: 'Bring it into the here and now. Say to the doctor, "You're not God." '

SAM: 'You're not God. I know that, but you don't, and boy do I hate you. Listen you filth, listen you slime, I'm a real person, not just symptoms – you darn well better relate to me as *someone*. You pig.'

IAN: 'Can you tell this pig some of your reality as a person? He is really listening now.'

SAM: 'This is me, I'm a real person, I'm hurt and that's why I'm here. I don't just need mending physically, I need mending emotionally. I need to be talked to. I need to be treated like a rational, intelligent human being. I can understand what you're talking about at the end of the bed, I'm not a twit. It's *my* blinking body you're talking about, it's *me, me, me*, you're talking about. I'm so frustrated.'

At this point in the dialogue, and with an eye on my watch, (time is limited) – I decide to use a 'dual control car' approach with Sam. We both have a hand on the steering wheel. Sam is already through his impasse, but where to go next?

A new growth area

IAN: 'Speak to the bat: "You are my frustration." '

SAM: 'You are my frustration. Being stuck in this hellhole and being absolutely powerless.'

IAN: 'Become the bat and speak back to Sam, "I screw you up, you need me." '

SAM: 'Do I? I'd be a damn sight better off without you. I need to respond and get things out of my system.'

IAN: 'Tell the bat how you intend to use him. Tell him the difference between frustration and expression.'

SAM: 'I'm going to use you to let me act more forcefully in those situations, to make the situation not as bad as when I was in hospital.'

'I can use you to shape my situation. I'm not powerless with you now.'

'I tell you, anger, I don't want to have you as a cudgel, you're for changing the situation. I want to have love and dialogue. I don't just want to be passive and done-to. But I don't want to do it through rage and fury either.'

IAN: 'So there is an alternative way of approaching life and doctors?'

SAM: 'Yes.' (Cautiously)

'It does not deny the first message to say I'd rather live by love. If I can really hate, I can really love with all that same energy and passion, with just the same clout. He, God, turns the wrath of man to his praise.'

IAN: 'Sam, you take authority over your wrath, choose whether to go on hating doctors or . . . – you complete the sentence.'

SAM: 'Or, I forgive them.' (Smiles broadly.) 'I'm smiling at the thought of going into hospital and loving the doctors, it hadn't occurred to me before. I'm just thinking through forgiveness.'

IAN: 'Yes, think through, "Love your enemies", it's a possible new growth area.'

A glance round the group revealed rapt attention for the last part of Sam's work. It was quite different to the look of bored frustration with which we all began. We were now united. It felt as if we were of one heart and mind with Sam in his predicament in hospital and his forceful expression of it to what appeared to be an uncaring medical regime. We all stood with Sam on the threshold of an adventure of interior change. The way ahead looked exciting with possibilities of an inner reconciliation, possibilities of understanding why they wore that garment of seeming aloofness and detachment and, who knows, possibilities of genuine forgiveness; an appreciation of medical people as fellow travellers on a similar journey.

The joy of this new possibility was anticipated in the group itself and in the next session, Molly, my co-leader who is a doctor herself, offered directly to Sam a heartfelt apology on behalf of the medical profession, for what he had suffered by their neglect of him as a person and their inability to comprehend the emotional components accompanying physical trauma. An apology with a straight request for forgiveness is an amazingly healing and life-giving gift. Molly's exchange with Sam had all the quality of a revelation, it had power to melt and to reconcile and to move into those new possibilities for the future.

Sam had strong defences to prevent himself getting into the danger area. At first I felt like a D-day landing force trying to cross a beach covered with buried mines, barbed wire entanglements and concrete blocks. Notice, too, the strong *projection* on to me of Sam's feelings about doctors and other professionals who had been involved in his treatment a year or two ago. In the face of his requests for real personal friendship, I needed to be very truthful about what could be offered in the limited time of one session. Our contract had to be based on, 'What is it you wish to do with your time here and now?', rather than any unlimited guarantee for the future. Sam had to struggle with this issue – how to use what is actually on offer.

The turning-point was his willingness to work, which became obvious on his return from the loo break. This willingness seemed to set me free to come alongside in a servant role, to make as strong a contrast as possible with the previous role-play of the 'professionalism' of the doctors.

I expect there are medical explanations for the violent twitching and drumming of the otherwise paralysed legs and feet. The emotional component of such an involuntary movement became very apparent during the work.

In conclusion, 'anger is anger is anger'. As a feeling, it is morally neutral. When hidden and denied it becomes a consuming fire and when St Paul says, '*Be angry and sin not*', I take it to mean, 'do not hide it'. But, I do not take him to mean, be as destructive and vindictive as you can. We all know the warlike and dangerous possibilities of unbridled rage and fury. Anger needs to be owned and recognised as the real feeling coming up now. We need to hear and recognise the message we attach to the feeling (in Sam's case, 'I hate all doctors, I loathe the way they treat me', etc). We need with equally clear deliberation to *change* that message by an act of will. We can renew our mind. For example, here is a new avenue of thinking for Sam about his experience: 'Certainly I was angry at the way I was treated, but I need not harbour that resentment for ever. I can express the frustration and get the anger out of my system. I can forgive, I can seek to understand how it feels to be a doctor with so many tragic victims of accident and disease to deal with daily. Then I can choose to think of them as my friends and to grow in a feeling of love towards them.'

Thus the anger can be converted. The vicious circle of smouldering resentment and impotence is at an end.

HANDLING ANGER – METHOD-LEARNING FOR COUNSELLORS

Strong feelings blocked
produce an impasse. They are impenetrable defences. Group life was slowed down to snail's pace until we found ways to unblock. (Role-plays and encounter-bat)

Projections
Sam perceived my behaviour very negatively (just like those ****** doctors!). A projection 'puts out' on to the screen of the present moment a 'slide' of past experience. For Sam I became as powerful, as impersonal, as 'Godlike' as those other professionals – I incurred his (concealed) wrath and could not make progress until it had been uncovered and recognised.

Role-play

I played the projection for all I was worth to bring it all into present awareness: I also played the opposite role – a helping servant figure – to free myself and to free Sam to put his wrath where it needed to go, i.e. towards the cushions representing the doctors.

Reversals

are fun, as well as very releasing. Thus from 'tin god' I moved to kneeling helper. From feeling 'scorned' by the medics, I urged Sam to switch and to scorn *them*. From his weakness and passivity I encouraged him to move into his strength and flaming anger. Both sides of the polarity need to be explored fully before the resulting synthesis can be approached.

Questions

Fritz Perls calls questions 'hooks'. When Sam asks about our relationship, 'What's the point of it?' I could get side-tracked into lengthy explanation. Instead I ask him to turn the question into an 'I statement'. This strengthens him to make a demand or a request. It keeps the initiative on *his* side. 'I want to be somebody special.'

Objectify

Instead of talking *about* anger in an abstract way, objectify it. We let the red bat 'become' Sam's anger. He was then able to see it, dialogue with it, and deal with it construc-tively. Always talk *to* rather than *about*!

Transformation

Powerful anger can become powerful love. The Spirit is willing . . . and waits for our willingness.

BRINGING IT HOME

1. Is there anyone at present with whom you are really angry? Or anyone with whom you are not prepared to share very much (concealed anger)? How could this situation be overcome?
2. If there is a circumstance in which you feel robbed, misunderstood or frustrated? Do you:
    (a) Suppress and deny it? (passive aggression)
    (b) Express and enjoy it in a hurtful way?
        (bitterness, malice, resentment)
    (c) Turn it in some way into creative energy for new life? (a recycled emotion!)
3. How can I make connections between my life and the mysterious words of Scripture below? In the light of these verses is it wrong:
    (a) To show anger?
    (b) To hide anger?
    (c) To feel anger?
4. As a Christian, how can I '*be angry and sin not*' (Eph. 4:26)?

SCRIPTURE

Matthew 5:21–6 (RSV) (Jesus goes much further than the law in Deuteronomy: he seems to overturn 'commonsense' attitudes.)

> '*You have heard that it was said to the men of old, "You shall not kill; and whoever kills shall be liable to judgement." But I say to you that every one who is angry with his brother shall be liable to judgement; whoever insults his brother shall be liable to the council, and whoever says, "You fool!" shall be liable to the hell of fire. So if you are offering your gift at the altar, and there remember that your brother has something against you, leave your gift there before the altar and go; first be reconciled to your brother and then come and offer your gift. Make friends quickly with your accuser, while you are going with him to court, lest your accuser hand you over to the judge, and the*

judge to the guard, and you be put in prison; truly I say to you, you will never get out until you have paid the last penny.'

Luke 6:27–31 (RSV)
'But I say to you that hear, Love your enemies, do good to those who hate you, bless those who curse you, pray for those who abuse you. To him who strikes you on the cheek, offer the other also; and from him who takes away your coat do not withhold even your shirt. Give to everyone who begs from you; and of him who takes away your goods do not ask them again. And as you wish men would do to you, do so to them.'

Psalm 76:7–12 (RSV) (God's anger against oppression and injustice however is something to be reckoned with.)
But thou, terrible art thou! Who can stand before thee when once thy anger is roused? From the heavens thou didst utter judgement, the earth feared and was still, when God arose to establish judgement, to save all the oppressed of the earth. Surely the wrath of men shall praise thee, the residue of wrath thou wilt gird upon thee. Make your vows to the Lord your God, and perform them; let all around him bring gifts to him who is to be feared, who cuts off the spirit of princes, who is terrible to the kings of the earth.

PRAYER

Help us Lord not to sin when we are angry
not to hide it –
not to exaggerate it –
not to keep a hidden score-card of wrongs and hurts.
Forgive us our trespasses as we forgive those who trespass
   against us.
Lord, turn our wrath to your praise. Amen.

FURTHER READING

Meaning in Madness by John Foskett (SPCK 1984): pp. 5–64 give transcripts of pastoral conversations in hospitals. Helps to distinguish pastoral care from counselling. Emphasis on need we have for supervision.

The Violence Inside by Paul Tournier (SCM 1978): N.B. Chapter 8: Violence in Others and in Ourselves; Chapter 9: Depth Psychology; Chapter 10: Hidden Violence.

Chapter Eight

ELIZABETH'S STORY – THE GIRL WHO PLAYED HIDE AND SEEK

I HAVE OFTEN thought when interviewing for a job, how good it would be to see the candidate's inner world. The track-record, qualifications, references and ability to come across convincingly in an interview are one thing: 'the inscape' – the balance of voices playing their eternal tapes in the inner living-room – may be quite another. It is the *inner* world which will actually create the 'magnetic-field' of emotional response around the person appointed to do the job. If the inner space is full of criticism or confusion then that is the atmosphere which will be increasingly experienced by colleagues and subordinates alike. The girl we work with in this chapter would be the first to support feminist causes and, in particular, women's ministry. The *real* liberation however begins within when she finds freedom to respect herself as a woman and to give and receive the things of God. Paradoxically the process begins when I offer a calculated insult to her femininity to bring about a sudden U-turn in the whole session.

I knew that Liz came from a strong, supportive Christian fellowship where she had no obvious leadership role. I did not know her full background story which will come out later in her follow-up letter.

Liz is an attractive, married woman of twenty-eight with dark curly hair. She wore a red boiler suit over a green top.

I found that working with her nearly exhausted my patience, illustrating once more that the bigger the resistance the bigger the blessing. It was as if she invited us to try one approach after another, then at the last moment we found ourselves in front of a brick wall. Isn't this just our own experience so often with inner difficulties – we get so far in the struggle and then find we cannot move, we cannot get through.

This is the notorious 'impasse', the place at which all our best efforts founder, all our trying seems doomed to failure. The turning-point for Liz was a moment of dramatic confrontation. In doing this the helper always risks the possibility that the work will stop at that point. In Liz's case she had the courage to pick herself up and try again, and this time we *were* on the move at last.

After this point it seemed that our human skills were at an end and God took over, moved in and finished off a situation we as a group could not see a way through. Yet we were there to be used and this faithfulness was all he needed.

I want to give only extracts of the dialogue, following it with Elizabeth's own letter written a month after the events narrated here.

Security operations

IAN: 'Well, Liz, you look quite determined to get through something today.'

LIZ: 'Not naturally, I don't know where to start. I want to talk about my attitude to myself, I don't like myself very much, I don't like other people, I don't like God very much, I don't like living with myself. I seem to contract inside, I've got a strong self-consciousness I can't get away from, I'm very negative.'

IAN: 'How do you feel about this group of people now, today, us?'

LIZ: 'Well, it's a very big group, I feel a bit lost.'

IAN: 'Say to the group, "You are too big, please be

smaller." But be careful, if you say it, we shall move closer, *is* that what you want?'

LIZ: 'I was almost going to say come closer. Come closer.'

I ask Liz to stand in the middle of the room and to invite group members she feels 'comfortable' with to come closer. She responds hesitantly as if fearful to offend anyone by saying what she really wants. Three people eventually position themselves nearer, to Liz's satisfaction. While this is going on I find her glancing at me as a schoolgirl might look at a teacher for frequent reassurance.

LIZ: 'Ian, I'd like you to stay.'

IAN: 'Are you saying, Ian, please be my security? Try that.'

LIZ: 'Ian, please be my security.'

IAN: 'No, I'm not going to be your security, you have security within you, so feel your own security. How would you feel safe? Liz, find someone you feel safe with and say, "I feel safe with you, stay in the group please."'

Liz does this to one person.

IAN: 'Can you extend that to anyone else?'

LIZ: 'I'm going to ask you to stay.'

IAN: 'You say, "I'm safe with you", but we all want to be free to be ourselves and unpredictable. You feel safe with three of us in this group yet we're not committed to being your security.'

I feel it necessary to prevent Liz investing her total strength and security in the group. She has her own strength and source of love within herself; it is this we are seeking. Somehow I am already becoming wary of a dependency situation where I (and the group) will find ourselves *responsible* for trying to help and failing! Many depressed and depressing people have a large collection of the scalps of would-be rescuers, fastened around their belts.

At one point Liz remarks in her schoolgirl voice that if she doesn't hold on tight 'something bad is sure to happen' – people will let her down, God will seem to back away too, she will let herself down – and him. The argument is

invincible, approach it how we might. Eventually Liz agrees
to a trust exercise, and discovers she *can* after all trust four
people with her weight – they don't let her down.

She allows herself to fall limply into the arms of the waiting group who are close enough simply to pass her from one
to the other. The exercise is designed to help her trust grow
as she allows us to take her weight completely and move her
on. Liz reports that she feels comfortable with this exercise.
I invite her to be lifted by the four people who have promised
that they will not let her down, and very slowly and gently
we lift her from the floor to shoulder height and rock her.
Liz reports after this experience.

LIZ: 'I didn't like it. I felt helpless, I wanted to struggle
               to be free. I didn't like your faces looking down,
               it felt macabre, it was like being dead and caught.
               It was funereal, those faces looking down. I
               wanted to struggle and stand upright, I didn't
               like being horizontal. I want to sit up, I am at a
               disadvantage down here.'

The rabbit hole

IAN: 'Be comfortable in any way you wish.'
LIZ: 'I still feel smaller with everyone around me.'
IAN: 'I suggest you make yourself bigger; stand on a
               chair and look down on us.'

Liz is experimenting now with different postures – too
low, too high, too exposed – nothing feels quite right.
(Remember her inner self is hiding down a rabbit-hole all
the time so how could *any* external posture feel 'right'?)

The next fifteen minutes or more could be described as
coaxing the rabbit. I tried to encourage her to share something of her secret self with one of these 'trusted' group
members. I failed dismally. At one point I thought, 'This is
it'. I reassured Liz that whatever she revealed about herself
or her past I would not hate or despise her. She declared that
she would have another go. I prayed eloquently.

IAN: 'Lord Jesus, by your Spirit give Liz now the grace
               and ability to see those secrets out there for just

what they are, just facts. Lord, please break the power of the past of darkness and secrecy to move us into light. In your name, Jesus, we rebuke and banish spirits of guilt and shame, dread and terror, which accompany these secrets. We tell them to get lost. Amen.'

IAN: 'I suggest that you begin by talking *to* the secrets. "I've been keeping you hidden because . . ." '

Long pause.

IAN: 'Is it okay?'

LIZ: 'I find it very difficult to imagine; I can't.'

IAN: 'I won't. "Can't" means "won't".'

Long pause.

IAN: 'What's happening, Liz?'

LIZ: 'I don't want to accept them, I don't want to.'

The pauses grew longer: I had challenged her to take responsibility for 'I can't' by changing it to 'I won't'. This threw up implications of obstinacy, deliberate refusal, stubbornness which were not lost on Liz or the group.

I produced three cushions and we agreed to let them represent the three 'secrets'. Liz felt an immediate aversion to them and refused to dialogue for long. 'I hate and want to kill you' gave us a clue about the violence inside and the need she had for her long delaying tactics. She spoke in terms of cutting, scratching, tearing, gouging. 'It's the sort of pain I feel inside – as if I've been cut up into little bits.'

The sinking ship

More long pauses follow, we have been at it nearly two hours and the group grows restive. Some are obviously 'switched-off'. One member complains:

'I'm becoming unhappy about that last exchange. You flick a glance at Ian, like the schoolgirl looking for approval. Have I got a good enough line this time to get by? I'm not convinced that you're really wanting to say something that's *you*, but only something that will adequately get by in the

group. I feel sad because I want to see you come
through to the truth for yourself.'

LIZ: 'Trouble is I don't want truth for myself, only
truth to satisfy other people, that's how it is.'

IAN: 'So, I want to please you all, fool you all and
deceive you all.'

LIZ: 'No, I don't mean that.'

IAN: 'Sorry, that's how I heard it.'

LIZ: 'That's not what I meant.'

IAN: 'Okay. Try to get more clear, tell me what you
do mean, "a truth to satisfy other people"?'

LIZ: 'I've felt often I'm the wrong person, I want to
be the *right* person, but it's not easy to find it.
Everybody expects that if you are a person,
ummmm.'

Liz begins to weep.

IAN: 'It's okay to cry. It's as if we're expecting a different person to appear. You have to pretend she's
here when she isn't.'

LIZ: 'But that's not real.'

IAN: 'So be real, Liz.'

LIZ: 'I can't be the person that people meeting me want
me to be.'

IAN: 'I can't live up to their expectations?'

LIZ: 'Not so much expectations, I don't think they even
expect a lot of me . . . etc., etc., etc. (!)'

Liz continues to bandy words now in a pathetic and snivel-
ling voice sensing accurately the boredom and annoyance of
the group. She even tries to end her work by looking at her
watch: 'Aren't we getting a bit late?' I avoid this manipulative
question by affirming the lostness, mystification and bewilderment now felt by the group.

It was as if Liz had to make a decision to abandon the
rickety craft she sailed, full of holes and listing dangerously.
Lifeboats had been hovering round but she would not jump.
Perhaps a torpedo was indicated.

IAN: 'The truth I'm coming to, Liz, is you *won't* work
tonight and you won't work *ever* and that you're
what's rudely called "a cock-teaser". You invite

attention and you back off, you invite intimacy then you close up, you make us all feel foolish sitting here, would-be helpers. Every offer you politely decline – "No I don't want to do that." So the game is, "Lead them up the garden path and then disappear." "Now where did she go? I thought we were getting somewhere." Then, "Where did she go?" and "Here she is – start again." "Help me." Then, "I won't do it", again, "I'll refuse again".' (Sighs.)

The garden path

LIZ: 'I can understand, I can't accept it.'

IAN: 'You find it unpalatable.'

LIZ: 'I do know in a lot of things I get to a point and I run away. As far as I know it's not designed to get attention, it's just I get to a point where I can't let go, I can't go through. I don't normally ask anyone to go that way 'cos I know that will happen.'

She sobs.

LIZ: 'It's not that I wanted to lead you all up the garden path, though if I was frightened I *would* do that.'

IAN: 'And what you feared has become your process. It's the story of your life.'

LIZ: 'That's why I don't normally let anyone near me, because I don't want to do that to them.' She sobs. 'So I'm not . . .' sobs again. *'That's what I do to God as well.'*

IAN: 'You keep him at arm's length. You invite him into your life and somehow you can't give it to him, you can't let go.'

LIZ: 'But I'm not a tease.'

IAN: 'You're not *wilfully* teasing us, okay, but *our* perception is we *feel teased*, not in a funny sense, but bewildered, we don't know where you've gone. Where did she go? Hide and seek is a better way

of putting it. One minute there she is, and the
next she's gone.'

Liz is visibly shaken by my comments, wants to deny
them. I suggest that she takes responsibility for what she
does (her process) and she decides to risk co-operation.

LIZ: 'So I can go back to one of those points and try
            again?'

IAN: 'Yes you can, Liz, only don't *try* this time, *do* it.'

Secrets that hurt

LIZ: 'I'll tell you something about myself that I don't
            want to. I had a sexual relationship with my
            brother when I was seven or eight and it went on
            for some time. And I've had other affairs since
            I've been married and I can't love my husband.
            Those are the three things I find most difficult to
            say.'

IAN: 'We're still here, still loving you. Do you sense
            some freedom now? What do you feel?'

LIZ: 'I still feel so bad about what you said about me
            earlier.'

She sobs again, and begins to play her familiar record
'Poor Old Me'.

LIZ: 'There are so many bad things that I didn't know.
            I didn't think there were any more bad things to
            know, thought I'd accepted them all and they no
            longer hurt.'

She sobs again.

LIZ: 'I always find worse things.'

IAN: 'You were so determined to be bad, you wouldn't
            even look at your goodness. Sorry, but I'm not
            going to believe that you're 100 per cent bad.'

LIZ: 'I know, but those things don't matter.'

IAN: 'The *big* ones matter, *they* run your life, rather
            than the good things you know with your head,
            like, "God loves me", "I'm a Christian". That
            seems to have no sway at all, but these others do,
                            these

three are knocking you about and cutting you up between them.

Liz, I want to say sorry about anything gratuitous in what I've said. I was desperate to sting you into some kind of response.'

Liz sobs again.

LIZ: 'It wouldn't hurt me so if it wasn't true.'

IAN: 'Okay. The hurt gives added validity. I'm not here to keep you safe, but neither am I here to hurt you, so at that point, sorry if I hurt unnecessarily.

Liz, what are you feeling right now?'

LIZ: 'I feel pretty crushed, stupid, but if there's one good thing I would have said it's that I'm honest with myself, which is obviously not now true so . . .'

IAN: 'You are, so far as you can see, but we often only see one tenth of the iceberg.

What do you want for yourself, Liz?'

LIZ: 'I don't know, I feel too tired.'

(We *all* felt tired but the session still felt unfinished. Two more challenges were necessary to get Liz finally to leave the sinking ship. One from me, the other from a perceptive group member, Charles.)

IAN: 'That's a cop-out – say what you want.'

LIZ: 'I just want to go to sleep for ever.'

IAN: 'In other words, "I want to die." How are you going to do it?'

Pause.

Victim needs rescuer

IAN: 'What goes on in the pauses?'

CHARLES, a group member: 'A big victim scenario is going on. She's playing victim.'

IAN: 'And I'm the rescuer. Well I'm not doing very well.'

CHARLES: 'I think there's a fixed, unfinished Gestalt: "I'm odd, I'm different, everyone else is okay, *I'm not*

IAN: – life is one big, self-fulfilling prophecy, I told you
so".'

IAN: 'Yes.'

IAN TO LIZ:'Charles is picking up the way you model your
life; you attract a rescuer, then stop him in his
tracks, cutting off his power.'

LIZ: 'Yes, that's what I do.'

IAN: '*I* feel quite impotent, don't know what to do with
you, or about you. I'm caught because I said that
I won't let you down. But there was an escape
clause, "as far as I am able", I'm not able to save
you to the uttermost, only Jesus can. I can suggest
things you might do and so far, with a few excep-
tions, you've refused everything.'

LIZ: 'So the things I've refused are to talk to people,
say my good points, what else?'

IAN: 'Those two will do for now.'

LIZ: 'Is it better to go back? I don't want to leave them
as refusals. I want to move back.'

Liz was now clearly willing to do the things she had been
refusing to do hitherto. That meant she was through the
impasse. It seemed to me an unnecessary labour to recapitulate the work with all the leadings, promptings and directions
she had refused. Instead, I asked her to stand on a chair and
play God, looking down on Liz and her situation and to hear
his word. As 'God' looked down on the cushion representing
Liz I placed upon it a crucifix, asking God to see her through
the finished work of Jesus Christ. The words of God the
Father to Liz (and through Liz) were very moving and
expressive. She gives some account of them in her letter.

It seemed to all of us that only a real experience of the
Holy Spirit could establish her firmly in the love of God her
Father, which she had now begun to receive. We invited her
to rest in the Spirit, providing a mattress to catch her fall.
She said that she was very willing and was in fact overwhelmed by the Spirit of God. She rested for some ten or
fifteen minutes in a quite altered state of consciousness, aware
of us, but also, and overwhelmingly, aware of the love of
God filling her and surrounding her. She received reassurance

of forgiveness for those things which she had been reluctant to speak about. The group gathered round her in fervent prayer and praise and Liz was aware of being an unselfconscious part of this worship.

Her openness and receptivity to God's love was to continue throughout the week.

A long and frustrating session had turned into a glorious triumph of the God-of-signs-and-wonders.

A letter from Elizabeth

Dear Ian,

Firstly, a very big thank you for the Gestalt Week, for all that it has meant to me. It was a very tough time in some ways, but also very exciting and productive. Despite feeling very bewildered at the beginning and a bit out of place among so many mature Christians with responsible ministries, the whole atmosphere of loving freedom and acceptance made me feel a far higher degree of peace and security than I would have thought possible under the circumstances.

I had experienced deep emotional problems for many years and had had a number of bad periods of depression. I had been very depressed for about two years continuously, and had felt increasing spiritual hopelessness for a number of years. Although, since my conversion at thirteen, I had always been aware of the activity of the Holy Spirit and had been touched quite deeply on a number of occasions, I felt I was missing the depth of intimacy in my relationship with the Lord which I longed for and which others seemed to experience. Worship had become painful and I nearly always left a church service feeling more cut-up and defeated than when I had gone.

I had known the Lord working in my life in a definite way through counselling in a 'Wholeness through Christ' prayer school and through the visit of a 'Vineyard team'* to our church last autumn. But subjectively I felt as if I was totally disintegrating – the more I tried to open up to the Lord the more I seemed to fall apart.

* An evangelistic and healing group under John Wimber.

I had also been seeing a clinical psychologist regularly for about five months, having been referred to him by a consultant psychiatrist who I had seen the previous summer when I was quite 'ill' and who had made a snap diagnosis of 'moderate manic depression', but listened when I said that I had found drug treatment unhelpful and that I was more frightened by the destructive nature of what went on in my mind when I was depressed, than by the misery of the depressed mood and the related physical symptoms.

My psychologist, although not a Christian, is a very warm, open, non-dogmatic person and has helped me to begin to identify what I was doing and saying to myself when I was depressed. He did not accept that I was 'mentally ill' in the medical sense, as the psychiatrist had implied. Which was in one sense a great relief, but in another sense was very disturbing as it put all the responsibility back in my court. In *my* terms it was 'all my own fault'.

I had a terrible time at work the week before I came to Scargill and ended up breaking down in a very humiliating fashion in front of a number of my colleagues, convinced that I could not cope, was utterly useless, and expressing this to my boss. On one level it seemed pretty pointless going on the course, except that it offered a temporary escape from equally difficult situations at home and at work, and that somehow there was a desperate hope that the Lord, however little I understood what he was doing, had directed me towards the course for a purpose.

As I was in your group and you will have much of my session on tape I will not give you a blow by blow account of what happened. Initially my reaction to all that happened before 'the breakthrough' was that it was all a waste of time, and to feel immense shame about that. I did find it very, very difficult and painful and found it very hard to be blamed when I felt that I was trying very hard. I didn't feel that I *could* be any other way. It clearly wasn't good enough and wasn't working. Part of my very problem was that I had always lived my life secretly, within myself and not out there in the real world.

Looking back at my 'script' I did raise several things, but

what was going on did not seem to ring true, I seemed to be continually missing the mark, and began to get panicky, feeling that yet again it would not work and I would fail. I suppose that is where your accusation that I was teasing you all did the trick. I was very deeply shocked and hurt and I both experienced and expressed that pain. I felt so condemned that nothing else seemed to matter, the sharing of my silly, sordid little secrets seemed almost irrelevant in the face of being exposed as an empty sham. The awful thing that I had feared would happen and which I always tried to protect myself against had happened and, as I saw it at that moment, someone had looked into my very soul, I was exposed as ugly and worthless. From that moment on I was very little aware of the group and it no longer mattered what they thought. I would do anything, and thus I was willing to share the secrets and to talk to my father, mother, brother and husband. Even that was not very deep, although all I said was true and at times upset me. Underneath was the deeper thing of being exposed and condemned.

That's why I went back to apologising for messing people around and to say to you that I was glad you'd been hard on me, that I found it so unhelpful when people were kind and comforting and gave me loving and comforting messages from the Lord.

What I wanted and expected was for the Lord to put his finger on where I was wrong and at fault and say, 'There, that is what is wrong with you.' I must have started jabbing and pointing my finger in condemnation because that's when you told me to *play God and speak to Liz*. And that's when the thing really went into top gear.

As I stood up and spoke to the Liz-cushion I vented some of my frustration with myself. 'It's your fault that you can't love me, because you won't, and you won't receive what I have for you.' That's when you put the crucifix on the cushion, and I don't know what happened, but it was the most wonderful thing that has ever happened to me. I was not saying what I knew I *should* say; I could have said words of love and acceptance with my mind and not with my heart, if it had come only from me.

I spoke words that can only have come directly from the Lord and because of that I profoundly believed and accepted them. Because I spoke them to myself and knew that they came from the Lord and were not merely motivated by the compassion of another person, they reached me in the way that all the prophecies and words of wisdom, etc., shared with me by another could not have done.

You went to take the cross away and I could not have borne it. That's when I said, speaking in my role as 'God', 'Liz, you are not the things you want to be, but you are the things I want you to be. You are my child because I made you. You are my bride because I bought you. You are safe because I've put my arms around you. She's small so I can hold her in my hands. She's special and precious.

I can accept you.

I can love you.

Liz, I love you.'

Looking at it dispassionately they are not very profound or original words, they are obvious and full of clichés, but they are words I would have previously shrunk from saying or hearing and then, and now, they were real and true and life-changing.

After that it seemed quite natural to ask to be inwardly filled with the Spirit, although I was very frightened that I would simply fall back and not be able to hold on to what I had seen and experienced. It was such a comfort to continue holding on to that cross. (Once it had all become for real it seemed very important to stand up, sit down, hold on to something, etc., to act out to a limited extent what was going on inside.) After that I am not at all sure what happened, I wasn't very aware of anything, although I knew that I had surrendered myself absolutely and that I had not been rejected or let down. I was completely overwhelmed.

Although I was not able to speak in tongues that evening when you anointed me with oil, that came quite naturally the following evening as I lay in bed, when I also had a little 'vision' of the glory of God in a middle-eastern sort of temple and was given words about my life being the temple where God's glory would dwell.

On the Thursday morning when John Bedford led the time of worship I was also able to join in the singing in tongues for the first time, which was a very special experience. I have often wept inwardly when others have sung in tongues and have felt shut out and left behind – earthbound.

During the month since the Gestalt Week some of the effervescent joy and slightly bumptious confidence has worn off – just as well as I felt a bit like Tigger in *Winnie the Pooh* and had to watch that I didn't upset people by 'bouncing' all over them. Despite some failures and set-backs and a very painful experience at work only a week after the course, which involved a very personal rejection in a relationship and an attack on my personal competence at my job, I have felt a new depth of peace and freedom. I have found that prayer is a quite different experience and a real source of strength. The Word of God has come alive again after years of dryness and boredom. I am experimenting in saying what I feel and mean, and have found that it has sometimes worked beyond my expectations and has never produced the dire results I feared.

I was able to share quite a bit of what happened during the week – including sharing the 'secret' about the relationship with my brother – with my husband, and as a result of my greater openness there has been a marked, if undramatic improvement in our relationship. As I am more willing to ask for help or genuinely to share my problems and emotions, John has been far more openly caring and cherishing.

My clinical psychologist has seen a big improvement in my mental and emotional state, and I shared a certain amount with him about the week, although I did not share much of the spiritual side, as he was clearly uncomfortable about that. This in itself was a big step, I rarely share anything with anyone, unless I have a cast-iron guarantee that they will accept and approve what I have said. Although cautious he was generally encouraging.

I still feel there is a very long way to go and I've got a lot to work on. I still find it difficult to believe that anyone, other than my very closest friends, will not reject me unless

I'm very careful about what I say and do. But being so much more aware of what I'm doing and *why*, I can confront those deep instincts and challenge them with the help of the Lord. I still find myself telling myself, 'You're a failure, you're useless, you're ugly, you're a real cow', etc., etc., but instead of accepting that condemnation I do now say, 'No, that's not true', almost at once. In the traumatic experience at work I allowed myself to feel really hurt and to accept my responsibility for my actual failures, while not accepting unreasonably the total blame for the situation. I did not seek to escape the pain by a blanket condemnation, 'You're hopeless', and a withdrawal into total depression.

For once, faced with an almost unbearable situation, as I experienced it subjectively, I did not want to die. However bad it felt at the time I believed that the future was worth living, and given a chance to escape I would still have chosen to go on. (I had for a number of years kept a reasonable stock of anti-depressants, etc., 'just in case'. The idea that I could have taken that way out if it all got too bad was a sort of insurance policy, although I doubt in all honesty whether I'd have had the courage to kill myself, much as I often wanted to die. The Friday afternoon that I got home they were all flushed down the toilet and I have not regretted it!)

This probably sounds pretty feeble and small-scale, but I am really rejoicing in how precious the Lord has become. I have found being able to look back over the script of my session really helpful, although I still find it very painful. I feel like one of the early arrivals in heaven in C. S. Lewis' *The Great Divorce* – almost invisible and not substantial enough for the bright, hard, strong reality of heaven. The very blades of grass hurt one's feet, but it is infinitely preferable to the grey, uniform awfulness of hell.

I wrote a poem two years ago in the early days of this last bout of depression:

From where does the emptiness flow?
Does it rush in and invade the soul or
well up from deep within?
In the deepest throbbing heart of darkness and pain

is there being or infinite absence?
Do I struggle on the circumference,
The tightrope-walker placing one foot in front of another,
the thin crust above the crater crumbling,
Or do I reach out my arms,
Whimpering in the vast womb of life?
Fathered and yet unprotected I lie.
'I' – 'I' – 'I' – that is the prison.
Oh – but to unbolt the door
And walk free from that cage behind my eyes,
Within my brain.
To see, to feel, to touch, to love
And not be 'I'.

I think that I am beginning to see, to feel, to touch and to love and yet to still be 'I'.

I'm afraid that this is not a short account, but long-winded, tedious and rambling. But lastly, I would like to thank you for your love, for the toughness which I found hard but tremendously reassuring and wonderfully freeing, and for all I experienced and learned just by being in that group. It was a tremendous privilege for which I am immensely grateful.

May the Lord richly bless you as you have shared his love and blessing with us. Thank you so much.

Love from
  Liz.

I would like to offer now what we have learned in this chapter in the form of a letter replying to Liz.

Dear Liz

Thank you for your account and your generously allowing me to use it for a wider public, with names changed. I must say the experience of working with you showed me yet again that when I am at the end of my tether and the group is at the end of its resources we can do no other than fall back on the grace and power of God alone. His strength was certainly made perfect in our weakness.

There were two turning-points it seems to me, two places where real repentance became possible for you, and you were able to say and *mean*, 'I am willing to change the way I am.' The first was after my confrontation with you when I pointed out some of the games you had been playing with me and the group. After that it seemed you had nothing to lose so why not do what was being asked? The second point came after your dialogue with the three secrets, when I asked you to see yourself from God's point of view. You soon spotted how he would be feeling about you, when every offer he made was refused and turned away from. It was clearly your own involvement in the encounter which brought these truths home to you. I doubt if mere reading or telling about such things would have had any impact for you must have heard these things a hundred times before.

I am glad you are going on in life, keeping the perception of new possibilities and new responses. This is the process we call 'renewing the mind'. You are learning to handle those accusing voices within you that have had power for so long to push you around.

Here are four steps and you can take them every time you hear the old negatives trying to re-assert themselves. They have well-built tramlines within you and a good deal of digging up and new road-making needs to happen. The work you have done needs to be followed up with very positive reinforcement.

STEP ONE *Disagree* with those long held, closely cherished lies (I'm ugly, I'm useless, I'm worthless, I'm the wrong person, etc.).

STEP TWO *Repent* for having believed them so long. Yes it really is a matter for penitence on your part, because in believing those things you are in effect denying and disbelieving the Word of God which has quite contrary things to say about his children. Don't miss out on this stage.

STEP THREE You can *negate* your negatives quite simply thus: 'I no longer need believe I'm ugly inside, useless, worthless, wrong, etc.'

STEP FOUR *Affirm* your positives, state your new position as a child of God strongly, tell the adversary what God tells you: 'I am special, I am precious, I am his bride, he bought me, I am acceptable in the Beloved.'

Do this daily and pray for continuous refilling of the Holy Spirit to live this way for today.

I am glad you are continuing in the appointments with your psychologist and that you feel more courage in speaking of the things of your faith to him. The real test, of course, comes with the observable improvement in your stability and ability to cope with life. God certainly doesn't want you down in the pit, but neither does he want you dancing all over everybody like a 'hilarious Tigger'. May he give you wings in your spirit to praise him and a level path with firm footsteps for your feet day by day.

Here are some verses from Psalm 40 (ASB) which reflect what I mean:

> *I waited patiently for the Lord and he inclined to me and heard my cry.*
>
> *He brought me up from the pit of roaring waters, out of the mire and clay and set my foot upon a rock and made firm my foothold.*
>
> *And he has put a new song in my mouth, even a song of thanksgiving to our God.*
>
> *Many shall see it and fear and shall put their trust in the Lord.*
>
> *Blessed is the man who has made the Lord his hope, who has not turned to the proud or to those who wander in deceit.*
>
> *O Lord my God, great are the wonderful things which you have done and your thoughts which are towards us.*
>
> *There is none to be compared with you. Were I to declare them and speak of them, they are more than I am able to express.*
>
> *As for me I am poor and needy, but the Lord will care for me.*
>
> *You are my helper and my deliverer. Make no long delay O Lord my God.*

Love, joy, peace to you,
    Ian

LEARNING WITH ELIZABETH :
COUNSELLING NOTES

The Impasse

Sometimes called the sick point. It is as if enormous walls of feeling confront and neutralise each other. There is a crack or crevice in between but it looks far too narrow to squeeze through. And who knows what's on the other side! It is the place where I am *stuck*. So much of me wants to keep it that way that it requires considerable determination, prayer and facilitator-skill to move me on. If I refuse to go through I remain stuck at the emotional age and stage when the original trauma happened. If someone persistently refuses to move it is usually helpful to end the session early and admit defeat. In Liz's case we took the different route of perseverance and prayer.

My Own Feelings

Impatience, frustration, bewilderment, exasperation, impotence were all present in turn. I need to be aware and in touch and ready to communicate them where appropriate. The counsellor has to be as *genuine* in the relationship as he or she expects the client to be.

The Unfinished Gestalt

refers to a kind of fixed immovable position to which we found ourselves always coming back with Liz. The road-blocks suddenly appear, *no way* can you continue! 'The victim' becomes 'the persecutor' and the 'rescuer' is immobilised or castrated. Once the routine is exposed for what it is, and renounced, progress is possible.

Revelation

The Spirit of God brought the session to a close in a way nobody could have predicted or planned, an illustration of humankind's extremity being God's opportunity!

Assimilation

Pay careful attention to the four steps above (Disagree, Repent, Negate and Affirm). Together they add up to *'the Renewing of your Mind'* (Rom. 12:2). They need to be deliberately done in the cool aftermath of a working session, later in the day or even a few days later. The steps are essential really to understand and to get hold of what has happened.

BRINGING IT HOME

1. How would you answer someone who asserts that healing and spiritual gifts are for others, but not for me? Or for *other* periods in history, but not now?
2. Ask your group to remember the fairy-tale of the prince and the frog. How many think of themselves *now* as princes (or princesses)? How many think of themselves as frogs? (If the question seems too embarrassing arrange for 'all eyes closed, hands up frogs, hands up princes'.) The 'score' will be an interesting fact of life!
3. Can you apply the scenario below (Rev. 12:10–12) to individual lives:
   (a) Elizabeth's?
   (b) People known to you?
   (c) Yourself?

SCRIPTURE

Revelation 12:10–12 (RSV)
And I heard a loud voice in heaven saying, 'Now the salvation and the power and the kingdom of our God and the authority of his Christ have come, for the accuser of our brethren has been thrown down, who accuses them day and night before our God. And they have conquered him by the blood of the Lamb and by the word of their testimony, for they loved not their lives even unto death. Rejoice then, O heaven and you that dwell therein!

But woe to you, O earth and sea, for the devil has come down to you in great wrath, because he knows that his time is short.

PRAYER

Father of all, we give you thanks and praise that when we were still far off you met us in your Son and brought us home. Dying and living, he declared your love, gave us grace, and opened the gate of glory. May we who share Christ's body live his risen life; we who drink his cup bring life to others; we whom the Spirit lights, give light to the world. Keep us firm in the hope you have set before us, so we and all your children shall be free, and the whole earth live to praise your name; through Christ our Lord. Amen.

FURTHER READING

On Becoming a Person by Carl Rogers (Constable 1974) – a classic by the founding father of non-directive or client-centred counselling.

A Tool for Christians Book 2 by Jean Morrison (Grigor) (Dept of Education, Church of Scotland, 121 George Street, Edinburgh, 1983): esp. Chapter 3 – Symbiosis – which deals with Persecutor-Victim-Rescuer scenario.

Healing the Wounded Spirit by John and Paul Sandford (Victory House 1985): esp. pp. 75–102 which include child-abuse.

Chapter Nine

CHARLES'S STORY: NOT SO STUPID AFTER ALL

W E LIVE TODAY in a scientific age. The world-view
we grow up with and breathe in from our earliest days has
no room for the supernatural. The world-view of Jesus and
his contemporaries was different. It was naturally supernatural! In order to move in spiritual ministries which obey his
instruction to 'follow me' we often have to re-educate our
minds. We may notice that a quarter of the space allocated
by the gospel writers to Jesus' healing encounters involved
taking authority over what he called evil, or unclean spirits.

In our day the same phenomena occur, and true to our
scientific world view we might call them idiopathic auton-
omous complexes. (It is as if part of the psyche behaves like
a little vortex of power with a mind of its own, controlling
the behaviour of its unfortunate possessor in antisocial ways.)

Jesus had an effective antidote: 'Get out!' It worked far
faster than pills or injections.

C harles is a large, genial man of 46, approachable,
friendly and warm-hearted. In any group of people you
would pick him out to ask him the way. He has a helpful
disposition and a natural attraction for the fair sex. He is a
Liverpudlian with strong working-class roots. He became a
Christian after marrying Alison when they visited a Billy
Graham rally. He's a man of many parts, a skilled artisan
with gifts of poetry, teaching and mature discernment in the
Spirit.

Charles has moved into much inner healing for himself

and has learnt to pray very effectively for others. But, he has always been dogged by a feeling of inferiority, a sense of being out of place even in a normal peer group.

He would express it succinctly, 'You can preach to others but still feel yourself to be a castaway'. Charles's work is brief, but deeply incisive. In a short time we move in and deal surgically with a crippling and long-standing personality defect. I encourage Charles to get in touch with the feelings he has in the present about belonging to *this* group. I then engage in close and trusting dialogue which is possible because of our previous association; the bridges of trust are already built. Charles is in touch with his feelings and the meanings of his bodily movements and sensations in a remarkable way. Towards the end of our time, I receive a 'word of knowledge',★ and a brief ministry of deliverance follows this spiritual discernment.

Charles looks uncomfortable and 'fidgety' as he begins.

The outsider

CHARLES: 'I want to face part of myself I'm not happy about. I often feel left out, left behind.'

IAN: 'Where do you want to place yourself this morning in the group?'

CHARLES: 'I'm happy where I am, on the edge here.'

IAN: 'Can we look at that, get in touch with being on the edge?'

Charles is silent for nearly two minutes.

IAN: 'What is happening, Charles?'

CHARLES: 'I'm on the edge, I'm not quite fully here. There are no deep feelings attached.'

IAN: 'What's it like?'

CHARLES: 'I feel that I'm here but not *belonging*.'

IAN: 'Would you work with that "not belonging" feeling? Would you get up and go round to each member of the group in turn and say something to each about not belonging?'

★ See Glossary (p. 185).

Charles rises and goes to each member of the group. To Jane – 'I don't belong'; to Tim – 'I don't belong, I'm not part of this, I don't fit, I'm not part of the group. In one sense I'm related to you but I'm different because of backgrounds, a different class, I'm from working-class. By your nature you're not.' To Bob – 'I'm different, completely. You can sum things up, you make me feel out of it.' To Liz – 'I do feel closer to you, but I don't belong in any shape or form. I do feel accepted by you, but I still don't fit.' To John – 'I don't fit, I don't belong, I see you as "establishment" and you Sam and Tim again, I'm seeing you both in as "establishment". That's what I feel.'

IAN: 'Stay with the feeling.'

CHARLES to Lillian: 'I feel insecure, I see you as having got things together, I see a sort of confidence in you. Confidence, it puts you "in" and me "out". That's not true, yet it *is* true, I can't move in.'

IAN: 'What are you in touch with?'

Charles starts choking, pauses.

CHARLES: 'I'm regarded as just a problem, judged, condemned, put down. It's like a tearing and breaking within me and I'm stuck with it.'

IAN: 'Show it bodily.'

Charles kneels down.

CHARLES: 'I want to hang my head, I can't go back, I can't go forwards, I'm stuck, there's like a rift – I'm pulled apart. There's this rift in my body.'

IAN: 'What is this being "pulled apart"?'

CHARLES: 'It's like an open wound.'

IAN: 'Feel it.'

Charles puts his hand over his heart and is breathing heavily.

IAN: 'Let some sound out.'

CHARLES: 'The sound won't come, there's a lump in my throat.'

IAN: 'Relax it.'

CHARLES: 'It's like a call, like "help me".'

IAN: 'Say it and say it again, exaggerate your call.'

CHARLES: 'Help me, help me, help me, help *me, help me.*'

Very heavy breathing accompanies these cries.

CHARLES: 'Oh, I've gone dizzy.'

Body language

The exaggeration seems to produce physical distress. The body is 'speaking' in its own eloquent way. I reassure the group that Charles is okay by asking him to rest, and ensuring that he keep in contact with me throughout his work.

IAN: 'Have a rest, Charles, keep in touch, look at me. You can go back in a minute. Have a break now.'

Charles is shaking across the shoulders.

CHARLES: 'I'm aware of tension, stiffness, my hands and arms are cold.'

IAN: 'Let the coldness take you over.'

Pause. Charles is breathing more quietly, his eyes shut.

IAN: 'What's happening now?'

CHARLES: 'I've sort of levelled off. I'm not acceptable, but also, I'm as good as anybody – you Ian, you Bob, you John, but different. I often can't do what's demanded of me, what you want.'

IAN: 'To whom are you addressing that Charles, "I can't do what you want"?'

CHARLES: 'It matters to me what you feel, it does matter what you think. But it also matters what *I* am, I don't *have* to conform.'

IAN (haughtily): 'You've *got* to do it my way.'

Here, I play devil's advocate for a moment. I want to provide stimulus, opposition. I am echoing voices from the past but I don't want to get identified with them for long.

CHARLES: 'Garbage! I'm not falling down on the job, how can I if I don't know what to do? So *help me, I don't know what to do.*'

Ian moves out of his seat and asks Charles to address cushions.

IAN: 'Let these be your parents, father, mother, all those who expected you to know, but never helped you, never told you what to do and gave you no model.'

CHARLES: 'He was my stepfather anyway. My real dad never came back from the war.

Fancy having such *stupid parents*, parents who don't tell you what to do.'

IAN: 'Use your fist, Charles.'

Charles thumps the cushions with great energy, perspiring and red in the face.

Tell it like it is

CHARLES: '*What am I supposed to do? What am I supposed to want? What am I supposed to be? Bloody stupid, bloody hell. God, they are thick. I think you're so bloody stupid.*

(Part of me regrets saying that.) *Sod the lot of you. Why can't you help me, help me to be, help me to see, to understand, help me to talk, listen to me?*

There's no way! I can't – I can't share with you who I am, what I am. They've not *begun* to understand me.'

IAN: 'Tell them.'

CHARLES: 'You don't understand me, I simply have to conform, but it isn't true, what about *me?*'

IAN: 'Tell them who you are.'

CHARLES: 'I've got a headache now.'

He breathes heavily, sits back on his haunches, sniffling, his face is very red and his hands are to his head.

IAN: 'What's happening?'

CHARLES: 'I'm waiting for it to subside.'

IAN: 'Talk to the headache.'

CHARLES: 'I want to close this eye, there's anger in my head.'

IAN: 'Become the angry headache. Say "I'm your anger, stifling you, choking you." '

CHARLES: 'I don't know what to say any more.'

IAN: 'Become the headache, talk as the headache.'

Charles's body convulses as he bends over and raises his fist. He seems to be choking with one hand on his stomach, he is coughing now as if to get something out.

Ian slaps Charles's back. Charles is breathing heavily, then kneels upright.

IAN: 'Take a rest.'

Charles wipes his eyes and says he feels easier, breathes more easily.

IAN: 'What's happening in your head?'

CHARLES: 'It's clearer.'

IAN: 'What's happening down below?'

Charles holds his diaphragm area.

CHARLES: 'I'm blocked. There's nothing coming from below getting through the block.'

IAN: 'Become the block and tell Charles what you are doing for him.'

Charles, speaking as the block:
             'I'm holding you back.'

IAN: 'Speak to your block.'

CHARLES: 'Why are you holding me back?'

IAN: 'Say what you'd do without the block. Try and find out why the block is necessary.'

CHARLES: 'You'd go too fast, you'd be too impetuous, you'd go off at half-cock, in the wrong direction.'

IAN: 'What's the name of your block?'

CHARLES: 'Hand-brake. You're not good enough.'

IAN: 'Call out to the block.'

CHARLES: 'But I'm as good as anybody, who are you? I feel the tension.'

A 'blocked' sensation usually means 'I am stopping myself feeling and expressing something. I give myself emotional constipation'. Charles needs encouragement to 'keep talking, breathing, feeling, stay in touch'.

IAN: 'Take a risk.'

CHARLES: 'I'm as good as you, but why am I in this state?'

IAN: 'Your feeling about not being good enough seems to be just the tip of something. Describe the tip as you feel it. Not good enough, the part that shows. Breathe down *below* the part that shows.'

Charles breathes deeply and dissolves into tears and coughing. It is as if he has received a body-blow and is almost 'winded'. The group feels and looks as if it has ringside seats at a heavyweight contest.

IAN: 'Let it all out from below.'

Charles coughs and splutters and blows his nose, looks more released.

'Hallelujah' – (he speaks in tongues).

A word of knowledge

IAN: 'Did you get a *word* for that feeling? I got a word as you were coughing – "illegitimate".'

CHARLES: 'My mother was illegitimate, I believe my father was too.'

IAN: 'I'd like to pray, Charles, for light in dark places. Is that okay?'

I pray a binding prayer over spirits of failure, inadequacy, illegitimacy, and ask the Lord to flush out what is painful and hidden.

IAN: 'You *kept* your anger with your parents, Charles, you didn't let it out. All that anger inside you will keep you ineffective.'

Charles prays a quiet, penitential prayer.

IAN: 'Start talking to your parents again.'

CHARLES: 'You *told* me – you never gave me a choice. That hurt me very deeply, but I want you to know that I do forgive you and ask my Father in heaven to forgive me for my resentment. But I'm going to do what is right for *me* as I have done, but it's hard work. Should I be feeling the anger? I feel sad for you both, and despair for you both. You were bigoted, you weren't open, you even ridiculed my faith. *You knew better.* I would have liked you at least to have heard me. The bigotry became a barrier, you would not listen. I feel sad because you and I missed out. I pray that the day may come when we communicate. I'm good enough to be the person I am, I don't have to live in the shadow of my father, I'm going to go my own way. I'm sorry for the grief, but I'll go the Lord's

way, I've been called into new ways, not your
ways, and I'm good enough. You always said,
"You won't make it", but I am good enough.'
I pray with authority at this point.

IAN: 'In the name of Jesus I cut you free from the stigma
in your parents' lives. I bind and banish those
negative spirits. Illegitimacy and Condemnation
leave now. Rejection and Inferiority *out*. Stupidity
and all Deceiving Spirits leave. Go where Jesus
sends you, harm nobody else, and never return,
in his precious name, Amen.'

Another chance

I invite Charles to do the rounds again.

He addresses each member of the group in turn. To Jane
– 'I belong here after all, I'm not on the edge.' To Tim –
'I'm from a different background but you can accept me, I'm
not stupid.' To Bob – 'I don't have to copy you, I have my
gifts, I can welcome yours.' To Liz – 'I feel close to you,
thank you for your love and support.' To John – 'Your
establishment doesn't threaten me, I need you too.' To Sam
– 'I can move in and out of your lives, I'm okay here.' To
Lillian – 'I can share your confidence, we're together in this
group. We're all just walking-wounded anyway.'

When someone has a gift of colourful and vivid expression
as Charles does and it is linked with the corresponding feel-
ing-content it is worth following closely, and allowing the
work to be steered by the speaker. Sometimes the speaker
will use bad language which might shock or offend us in
more usual social situations. It is recognised in a healing
group that this is a powerful channel of release. Such language often comes straight out of our pre-Christian past.
The group would in no way help if it began to register shock
or non-acceptance at points like this.

A new feature which appeared towards the end of Charles's
'work' was the expulsion of demons. During the coughing
and spluttering sequence it was as if the word 'illegitimacy'
flashed across the screen of my mind. Such a revelation is

known as a 'word of knowledge' and the corresponding ministry in a situation like this is to deal with the situation in the power of the Spirit and in the name of Christ. I therefore prayed with authority to expel the negative or contrary spirits that I discerned within Charles. For a fuller explanation of my understanding of this ministry of deliverance please see Chapter 12.

Finally, I asked Charles to 'do-the-rounds' again. This enables him to recapitulate the beginning of his work and to test immediately the efficacy of what he has been through. It gives a rounded off and closed feeling to the agenda of this episode in the group.

Some workers in this field prefer a finish which is open-ended, but I confess I prefer a sense of something completed, a definite, manifest achievement.

Charles wrote some months later that people noticed a 'change' in him. He had a quieter, more authoritative manner. He also reported that his hesitancy and inferiority feelings with groups of fellow ministers had disappeared.

CHARLES'S WORLD-VIEW – A LEARNING BOX FOR THE MINISTRY TO BODY/MIND/SPIRIT

Doing the Rounds
Meet and address each person in the group with eye-contact. Make a straight communication. Charles worked effectively in this way – at the start to express his predicament, and at the end to express his new position. Always a good exercise to bring us back to interpersonal reality.

Body Work
Charles's body 'spoke' by acting out his inner state. His symptoms and sensations were more eloquent than words. Dizzyness, stiffness, heavy breathing, choking, a feeling of rending, of blocking, shaking, flushing, perspiring, thump-

ing, splitting headache, coughing, are all ways of out-working the distress. Allow any one of these symptoms to express its meaning by imaginatively 'becoming' the symptom and enter dialogue with it (e.g. Charles was asked to *become* the headache, and later the block at his diaphragm). When any symptoms – physical or mental – look like taking over a client, call them back into contact with the facilitator and awareness of the group. Keep them in touch; tell them to have a rest. If someone seems to need to go into extreme physical weakness, keep them in touch alternately with their strength and the life principle within them. 'Come back into your strength!' This is the place from which such a person should work. Tread carefully – these areas of fantasy life are extremely powerful.

Sound Out
Inner tension and blocks are often released by deeper rhythmical breathing, and by encouraging the client to emit sounds on the out-breaths. 'Let your sound out!' Words and short phrases can often be repeated and exaggerated with great effect (again . . . again . . . louder, etc.).

Binding and Loosing
Another method of achieving release from tension and bondage. When prayer is appropriate use commanding, authoritative prayer – 'In the Name of Christ I bind . . . I loose . . . I release you' etc. When contrary spirits and negative 'complexes' have been discerned *and you know your client is ready to let them go* – pray them *out*, with suitable strength and authority (this does not imply shouting!). Address them directly like the vermin they are, 'I tell you to *go* in the Name of Jesus.' In psychological parlance the illegitimacy, rejection, stupidity, inferiority etc. were *introjects*, they had been 'pushed in' and needed to be 'coughed-up'!

BRINGING IT HOME

1. Are there things about you that, try as you will – admit, repent, confess – you cannot shift? What would Jesus have called such stubborn and contrary parts of our nature?
2. What was your family nickname? What was your reaction?
3. What was always said about you which stuck and hurt, though perhaps you never complained? (Charles was called 'thick', 'stupid', and told, 'You'll never make it'.)
4. Are there 'contrary spirits' in your life that might respond to deliverance prayer more readily than good resolutions? Are such things transmitted, inherited, caught or taught?

SCRIPTURE

Matthew 17:14–20 (New RSV)
  When they came to the crowd a man came up to Jesus, knelt before him and said, 'Lord have mercy on my son, for he is an epileptic and he suffers terribly; he often falls into the fire and often into the water. And I brought him to your disciples but they could not cure him.' Jesus answered, 'You faithless and perverse generation, how much longer must I be with you? How much longer must I put up with you? Bring him here to me.' And Jesus rebuked the demon and it came out of him and the boy was cured instantly.
  Then the disciples came to Jesus privately and said, 'Why could we not cast it out?' He said to them, 'Because of your little faith. For truly I tell you if you have faith the size of a mustard seed you will say to this mountain, 'Move from here to there', and it will move, and nothing will be impossible to you.'

Matthew 18:18–20 (New RSV)
  'Truly, I tell you, whatever you bind on earth will be bound in heaven, and whatever you loose on earth will be loosed in heaven. Again, truly I tell you, if two of you agree on earth

about anything you ask, it will be done for you by my Father
in heaven. For where two or three are gathered in my name, I
am there among them.'

PRAYER

Heavenly Father, whose blessed Son was revealed that he
might destroy the works of the Devil and make us the
sons of God and heirs of eternal life, grant that we, having
this hope, may purify ourselves even as he is pure, that
when he shall appear in power and great glory we may be
made like him in his eternal and glorious kingdom, where
he is alive and reigns with you and the Holy Spirit, one
God, now and forever. Amen. (Collect for Epiphany 6,
ASB)

FURTHER READING

But Deliver Us From Evil by John Richards (DLT 1974).
   Chapter 6 introduces the Deliverance Ministry and differ-
   entiates it from exorcism.
Heal The Sick by Reginald East (Hodder 1983): esp. Chapter
   12 'The Spirit and Emotional Healing' and his appendix
   on the Deliverance Ministry.

Chapter Ten

THE STORY OF THE GROUP AND WHAT HAPPENS AFTERWARDS

THE IRISHWOMAN was alleged to have said, 'How do I know what I think till I hear what I say?' She might well have added, 'How do I know who I am till I see the effect I have?' We are all members of *groups* from our earliest days and, for better or for worse, it is these groups which affect most deeply the kind of personality we develop, our self-image, and what we want to become. From the time of our birth into a family, most of life's activities involve *others*. Those others may breathe life and affirmation towards us or their effect may be toxic, their presence spell oppression and destruction.

Belonging to a group is not a panacea for all ills. Group life can be static, plain boring, or even oppressive. But a quick glance at the group-life around in society and in the church soon shows that where there's a purpose to grow and learn or a will to achieve something new, then you need a group of like-minded people, an input of resources and a leader.

In the church we find groups for Bible study, Lent-courses, confirmation, enquirers, discipleship, faith-sharing, prayer. There are very few solitaries in the Kingdom of God! The very word 'church' is meant to convey not a building, not an institution with a tradition, but a group of people! In the counselling world we find groups for encounter, sensitivity, training, growth, co-counselling, group-dynamics. In the world at large groups are forming for every addiction, condition or purpose imaginable, alcoholics anonymous, ante-natal, bereavement, battered wives, retirement, political, environmental. What makes a group tick? How does it stay together? How does it achieve its purpose in a satisfactory way?

This chapter examines the group life of the people described in this book and others like them.

How can I describe the atmosphere and ethos of the *group*? It amounts to something far greater than the sum of the parts. When nine people are prepared to learn new ways of being themselves and to allow the Holy Spirit to lead, it has the joy and freedom of a good summer camp, it has the strenuous, purposeful activity and intense loyalty of a good football or hockey team. It has all the humour, banter and harmony of a group of friends who love and trust each other. It can have the dedication and team-work of an operating theatre. It can experience the frustration of a class kept in after school or the shekinah glory of the Hallelujah Chorus. It can call forth reverence and awe: it can be experienced as a new way of living.

Two epic documentaries on television illustrated the intense 'belongingness' of groups in their respective situations. *Tenko* was the story of a group of women, prisoners of war in the Far East, and *Anzacs* traced the story of a battalion of Australians through the campaigns in the First World War. Both the sagas bore witness to an experience of group life which was greater than the sum of all the parts. These times were, for those who took part, transcendent, unforgettable, life-changing and thus it is for membership of a growth group.

I like to tell the newly-arrived group during the introductory session, 'Your group will be for this week your entire world, a small universe, consisting of eight other people in one room for nine sessions of between one and a half and two hours each. Nevertheless, in that small world, you will find in each other person a reflecting mirror and a resource of help. They will know nothing about you and yet in the sense that really matters, they will soon seem to know all about you. You will find it is a place to discover yourself. You will find, if you allow it to be, that it is a safe place. The other members of the group are like a safety net, so that when you do your tightrope walk you will not fall far. You will find it is a challenging place, a place where compromise and pretence have a hard time. You will find that it is a truthful place, but you will be safe to receive the truth and to speak your truth, because of the understanding and trust you have all established one with another.'

These may sound extravagant claims. I can make them with confidence because they have been borne out time after time, group after group. When I leave my normal surroundings and responsibilities, the commitment to my people in my ordinary life, I find for one precious week that I have a chance to be more real and essentially myself and to experience more of the reality and essence of others on similar journeys than ordinary routines of life seem to permit.

For this brief period I have the privilege of a place of intimate belonging, a place of provision and protection, a place of release and healing, for which my soul has been thirsting and longing.

There are as many styles of group as there are purposes for which people meet. We are all familiar with the classroom situation, sitting in rows or facing one way, power and wisdom vested in one person up-front with blackboard or overhead projector. We are all familiar with the small committee which works to a tightly arranged agenda and seeks for a common mind or a democratic vote. Some of us will have moved in the sixties into the fashionable encounter groups of the period. Here, there would be no agenda, the group would be encouraged by the facilitator to interact and allow the *group process itself* to be the learning and the experience. Thus we discovered bids for leadership, the tendency for fight or flight to take place, scapegoating, pairing, polarisation of groups – right and left, north and south, male and female, feelings of hostility to people outside the group and suspicion of those who were absent. We encountered each other, sometimes abrasively, sometimes with great affection, we formed alliances and hostilities, we learned about the ways in which we bore and frustrate ourselves in ordinary life, at first hand and at close quarters. These groups had their different emphases: T-groups were, and still are, in use in management training circles, encounter is sometimes 'hard' and designed to shock. Sensitivity groups are more useful for counselling training and aim to increase each member's awareness of the others and the group process. These have a softer encounter element.

Some groups are leaderless, some groups have a common interest or theme, such as single parents, alcoholics or hospital chaplains. The groups engender different leadership styles from the totally didactic at one extreme to the free-for-all of a 'leaderless' group at the other. Sometimes more learning takes place at the latter end of the spectrum than the former.

The group you have been encountering so far in this book I call a Christian Growth Group. The leadership role has a high profile, but as the week proceeds and people become confident in their own skills and strengths, this reduces and leadership is a function shared by more members in the group. Only occasionally do we spend time working with open group interaction. This may well appear towards the beginning of the week. Our more usual style is to invite somebody to step into the limelight and use the group's time and resources for their own personal benefit, as in each chapter, making clear their intention to work and spelling out as far as they can what it is they want to do. The group then becomes a resource of loving attention, sometimes prayer, sometimes role players for the different characters involved in a person's inner drama.

I make it clear to each person who wishes to work that the outcome is their *own* responsibility. In no way do I wish to programme them or set up hoops for them to jump through. My interventions are intended to facilitate their *own* process and to clarify what has happened. The group is available to them for the same purpose. The hidden bonus, however, the spin-off we all receive, is that each piece of work is 'cathartic' in some way for every person in the group. When we have seen a really first-class drama we feel inwardly cleansed, perhaps released in some way, we share the emotion of the actors on the stage or the film. They, by proxy, seem to work *for us*. In the same way watching someone work in a growth group will cause others in the group to identify in some way, and to share the experience. They all reap benefit from the work accomplished. The human predicament is, after all, not so very different from one person to another. The range of experiences, emotions and responses within the human lot may have an infinite variety of circumstances and manifestations, but is basically confined to a very few cardinal needs, experiences and reactions.

How strange then that each of us hugs our personal secrets so tightly as if no one else had ever felt this way! What a delightful surprise it is when these things have been shared, perhaps in fear and trembling, to discover that every other member of the group knows what we are talking about. Each one has shared our predicament in a way personal to themselves.

At the beginning of a group's life I ask each person to introduce themselves saying a little about where they come from, what they do and their family background. Soon this leads into an explanation of why they have come here this week. Do they have any particular hopes and are they prepared to share any particular apprehensions or fears they have as they enter a new group? I confess that I am always hopeful at the beginning of the week that someone will know quite clearly why they have come and be prepared to entrust themselves to a group of comparative strangers. When someone is ready within the group it means that we can get down to work quickly and the trust-building work looks after itself. If this does not happen at once we may spend one or even two sessions testing the water, questioning or even challenging the leadership, discussing matters arising from the lectures. The group has a need, step by step, to establish confidence, to learn to trust me and each other.

Eventually someone will offer to work and eight typical sequences have been described in this book so far. Sometimes this work will not finish with a good sense of completion, sometimes it will not even appear to have started in any depth. It may be possible later in the week for that person to have another innings. One or more members of the group may hold back and be unwilling to risk themselves in a situation which must seem at first like walking on the water. The leader of the group may have to face challenges and leadership bids from the more senior or experienced members present who might know other ways of handling this or that person.

At other times a member of the group may provide diversionary tactics – sitting in silence, coming in late, needing to change places or smoke, or leave the room for this or that reason. However, as I always mention, the door is never locked and anyone is free to walk out. Sometimes a group member will leave the course altogether because the inner pain of seeing others' work becomes too great to contain. I always invite such leavers to come again when they feel able to. Group members soon discover they have a contribution to make to the group; instead of being spectators they become active participants in the healing process. In primal work they may help in the quick assembly of a birth passage with cushions and pillows. They provide the pressure needed for the infant's head, they take on the roles of mother or father. Sometimes a group member will role-play Jesus. The simple presence and attention of the group *is* the facilitating environment. It enables things to happen and to happen quickly.

Towards the end of a session as we move towards prayerful closure, group members will have words of knowledge, pictures, Scriptures or prophetic words for the person concerned. In the composite group described in this book Charles was able to take over the leadership of the group for a complete session before the end of his particular week.

As, one by one, people do their work the anxiety level in the group, very conspicuous at the start, falls away to zero. By the mid-point it is as if we had known each other all our lives, and much humour, teasing and joyful exuberance are in evidence at meal tables. By the end of the conference there is a sadness that this particular 'world' is coming to an end. Often conversation will turn towards endings, closures,

death. In pairs, yet remaining in the group, I invite people
to review their work, picking out the main negative or
destructive elements which were uncovered in their session
and asking them, with their partner's help, to disagree, to
repent and to posit a new positive-faith judgement backed
up by a verse or a word from Scripture. This exercise, which
we call 'Renewing of the Mind', helps people to assimilate
what has happened and gives a substantial and almost tangible gangway back into life-at-home where the new learnings have to be applied.

The group will often end on a note of celebration. In one
group I heard corks popping as they shared cake and wine.
Another group led us into a dance at the final communion
service. One group gave each other imaginary presents
before saying good-bye – like a grand piano to someone who
had neglected his gift of music; like a holiday on a South Sea
island to someone who couldn't find the time to take his
family away last year; like a word processor and a well-
trained secretary to the busy minister whose study was in
perpetual chaos.

In conclusion I would like to call on several witnesses,
each to summarise their experience of the group and its
follow-up. I will use their own words as they come from
evaluation sheets or letters written sometimes long after the
experience. These extracts are written by group members
other than the ones you have already met in this book.
(Names have been altered.)

Peter writes:

'Here is a list of noticed benefits.

1.   I could link back to previous counselling training and
experience, both intellectually and emotionally [Peter had
done a University Diploma in Counselling and Guidance]. I
could build the new insights on to this previous sound base,
a nice feeling to be able to integrate in this way.

2.   Group work modelled new approaches linked with
the Christian faith, and enabled me to be more active in a
counselling approach to several people. I valued your varied
approach to different personalities. It enabled me to get into
meaningful 'cushion work' with others, enabled me to be

more assertive both on the week and on return. It was the biggest personal development experience for some years. It was a definite religious experience, I felt, 'I am his and he is mine', – a development of my experience of and submission to God.

Finally, greater confidence – it triggered a rethinking of the role of groups and my own eldership in my church.'

Catherine wrote:

'When my turn came for group work I worked on an aspect of my relationship with my mother. Basically she is a very domineering person and when we meet, only occasionally, I find it very hard to make adult communication with her. So essentially the tape to erase is, 'I don't exist', and replace it with, 'I am, I am me, Catherine'. The group helped me work on a possible approach to take in conversation with her. Okay so far but – three days after the conference ended – I spent a day with my mother and did not manage (choose) to interrupt her and stand on my own ground. It has made me realise my aims must be realistic and practical. Interestingly the one time I felt I had an utterly free choice was to give her a kiss on the cheek when saying goodbye – something I had done twice in the last thirty years – and there I truly regret I chose not to. But the 'I am' needs more working at. Everest is climbed by perseveringly putting one foot in front of the other. Having said all that it has helped me clarify in my mind what I'm aiming at in terms of the relationship.'

June writes:

'Getting your letter and questionnaire was, I now see, the final step in a series, since returning from Scargill, which has resulted in, for the first time that I can ever remember, my father and I communicating about feelings, and the first time I've ever heard him express and show his own feelings. It would take me too long to explain all the hows and whys here, but I can see some of the steps that the Lord has taken me through recently. They all move onward from the moment during my work time in the group, when the 'it's-*not*-my-fault' moved from my head to my gut level. I am thrilled by my new freedom (light and fizzy), but also sobered as I see how tightly the guilt and false guilt held me, even though I had been a believing Christian as long as I can remember, and there is such a lot more to learn.'

In a previous letter she had said:

'As we were looking up Scriptures for renewing the mind at the end of the last evening and you were helping us, you and Jerry and I stood in a group with Bibles and notebooks, then as you prayed you put your arm around me and being that much smaller than you I felt as though I was tucked in safely and could lean my head on your shoulder. I have never experienced that close, strong, sheltering hold before, especially, as you said, 'from a man-person'. I don't remember my father ever holding me.

'What was to me the special gift was that my picture of being with my heavenly Father has always been in exactly that way, sheltered under his wing, with my head able to rest at his shoulder when I want. You have ministered to me, in a new and more tangible way, the sense of God's fatherly care, to fill out the picture of his love which he has already given. As you had prayed earlier for a new awareness of the Father's love for me I received that moment as his answer and another miracle of his grace. "I thank God upon every remembrance of you", the group and all the Community.'

June says of the group work:

'I have never worked at such depth before and never have I felt such strong support from any other group. I believe this enabled me to reach a point of special significance for me. Learned much, both technical and personal, from the Gestalt work, but also the group work was very effective for me in many, many ways. Strong affirmation I found to be a very important upbuilding, and renewing of the mind was helpful:

1. Because it was the first time I had followed up immediately a new awareness with guided, practical, positive steps to put the new, inner knowledge out into planned changes in living.

2. Because sharing the task with another person who was close and with whom I shared common understanding as a

group member, enabled me to have extra self-knowledge reflected by him and it was completely acceptable to me, however hard to hear because of our shared experiences in the group, i.e. blunt observations from a trusted friend.

3.   Because this period of guided reflection on my work and its implications enabled me to locate aspects of my process which I did not understand and to get elucidation immediately from group members or facilitator.

4.   Because this experience helped me to put the old, negative, well practised scripts-to-be-changed and the new positive ones into their Scriptural context and to connect attitudes as explored in the group, with sin, repentance, forgiveness and rebirth as revealed in Scripture. Particularly this has moved my head level evangelical view of choice into a new and effective place, perhaps into my soul.

5.   Renewing the mind moved my whole focus of events back from myself where it was as usual after group work to my heavenly Father.'

My last witness is Carol. After describing briefly her work which set her free from what she calls her 'mallet-doormat syndrome' ('I either have to respond aggressively like a mallet, or I become too submissive like a doormat'), she mentions the group:

'Jesus was in the midst of the group and reassured me of his love. My brothers and sisters in the group expressed their love and care for me and I really sensed this support. Since I came home the changes in my life and attitude are as follows:

1.   Although I would not say that I am depressed my feelings have been very up and down. I seem to weep very easily and many fears have come to the surface. I am sure, however, that it is all part of the Lord's healing process. My husband, Ted, and I have laid down our work for the church at the moment, both as musicians and in counselling, as we believe our relationships with each other and the Lord are more important than any so-called ministry. Having said that, however, I feel as though I have been put on the rubbish dump (poor old me). This may sound very negative, but I

believe it to be necessary and as we remain open to the Holy Spirit I am sure he will do something beautiful with us.

2. God has enabled me to love the unlovely. A young man who was a practising homosexual when we first met him, to whom we had opened our home, ministered, loved and encouraged, decided to make a homosexual attack on our twelve-year-old son last year. I was devastated, but after bringing the situation before God in prayer, I decided not to kill him, but to be mature and forgive him. My feelings, however, did not fall in line with my decision and I could not bear to be in his presence or even see him. In church on the Sunday after Scargill this young man came to me, and to my surprise not only had the feeling of repulsion left me, but also my heart was filled with an overwhelming love for him. The Lord has truly healed the relationship.

3. At the end of the church service on the same Sunday the Spirit prompted me to go to a certain lady, one who had been very difficult under my husband's leadership, and tell her that I needed her love for my healing. At first I ignored this prompting as I didn't think it was a good idea, but eventually decided to be obedient and leave the responsibility with the Lord. When I said what I had to say she was deeply moved, she put her arms round me and told me how wonderful it was that someone other than her husband and children should need her love. Another relationship healed. During the weeks that have followed this incident she has made special efforts to be kind and I am sure that the work done in both of us will be an ongoing one.

4. I'm aware that my heart has been softened and that I am much less independent in my attitude. I realise now just how much I need my husband. Unfortunately he is locked in somehow and cannot give me the affection that I need. In fact he never has been able to. This has resulted in a part of me dying inside and my having to stand on my own two feet. As Jesus brings me back to life it would seem that I am in a kind of dilemma, because I now need something I cannot yet have. Again I believe that he has started a healing work in both of us in this area, and I know that he will not leave it incomplete.

5.   The feedback that I have had from other people has been quite positive and comments such as, "Is this the same woman?" and "You seem to have an inner tranquillity", keep coming. Several people have said that I look different, more calm and composed.'

The above letters are written weeks or months after the event. Experiences like the ones they describe can and should be part of the ongoing provision of the local church. When he began his ministry of announcing the Kingdom of God Jesus called together a small group. It was to be his inner world, the base camp from which to launch his mission and his healing. They were to be the ones who, by their close and intimate interaction with him, and each other, would eventually change the world. But how many of us have known that close and intimate interaction with a group of people, a group committed to each other, and seeking the Spirit for love and for truth? I believe it is the business of every local church to be providing such groups which, when functioning well, build the body, supply the ligaments, (i.e. the relationships) of trust, and act as a springboard for effective ministry and mission in the world. Of course I am not here talking about 'training groups' which will learn a ten-point programme for converting the individual or winning the neighbourhood back to God, important as these may be. I am referring to an ongoing healing, nourishing, servicing and maintenance work group where each Christian soul can be tended, cared for and refreshed by the others, where each can learn not only his or her own needs, but also his or her own resources-in-God and how to use them. I am talking about small outposts of heaven, little icons or glimpses into the everlasting qualities of that place where I shall know as I am known. And if the church is not in the business of preparing people for the life of the world to come, then, to coin another phrase, which our Irish lady might use, 'What on earth *is* it doing for heaven's sake?'

A LEARNING BOX : GROWING IN GROUPS

To establish a ministry group committed to personal growth and mutual support, you need:

1. A leader with some experience of group work and authority to minister in your fellowship or church.
2. A clear understanding on the part of all members as to what the group is about.
3. Between eight and twelve members. Too few means less resources and gives an exposed feeling. Too many crowds the room and makes avoidance of work more likely.
4. An agreed season: a residential weekend, or e.g. ten consecutive Fridays 8.00–10.00 p.m.
5. A firm commitment to attend, on the part of every member, 'come hell or high water'.
6. The ability to turn from 'in-reach' to 'outreach' frequently. Such a pastoral care/healing group as I have described should not become an end in itself, it must always be seen as necessary *'to prepare God's people for works of service, so that the body of Christ may be built up ... and become mature ... '* (Eph. 4:12–13, NIV). A parochial group established by clergy or leadership team might well function on the lines described here twice a year.

BRINGING IT HOME

1. It may be that a group using this book would like to develop into a growth-group. What steps would be necessary to achieve this object?
2. As an individual, what groups have been important in your life from childhood onwards (include present-day groups)? Make a list and score them on a 0–10 rating for the following characteristics.

(a)   Interesting.

(b)   Held my loyalty.

(c)   People I admired and sought to imitate.

(d)   I learned a lot.

(e)   I played a full and active part.

(f)   I found fulfilment in giving.

(g)   I felt fully involved and committed.

(Example of scoring e.g. *Scout troop* (a) 5 (b) 7 (c) 10 (d) 6 (e) 9 (f) 6 (g) 10 Total score: 53)

3.   Evaluate the 'group-life' scores of the different memberships you have moved through in life. In discussion short-list the qualities you are looking for in groups you join now and in the future.

SCRIPTURE
Group Life in the Early Church

Acts 2:1–4 (New RSV)

When the day of Pentecost had come they were all together in one place. And suddenly from heaven there came a sound like the rush of a violent wind and it filled the entire house where they were sitting. Divided tongues as of fire appeared among them and a tongue rested on each of them. All of them were filled with the Holy Spirit, and began to speak in other languages as the Spirit gave them ability.

Acts 2:44–7

All who believed were together and had all things in common. They would sell their possessions and goods and distribute the proceeds to all as any had need. Day by day as they spent much time together in the temple, they broke bread at home and ate their food with glad and generous hearts, praising God and having the goodwill of all the people. And day by day the Lord added to their number those who were being saved.

Acts 4:32–3

Now the whole group of those who believed were of one heart and soul and no one claimed private ownership of any possessions but everything they owned was held in common. With great power the apostles gave their testimony to the resurrection of the Lord Jesus and great grace was upon them all.

1 Corinthians 12:24–7
But God has so arranged the body giving the greater honour to the inferior member that there may be no dissension in the body, but the members may have the same care for one another. If one member suffers all suffer together with it. If one member is honoured all rejoice together with it. Now you are the body of Christ and individually members of it.

PRAYER

Worthy is the Lamb who was slain to receive power and wealth and wisdom and might and honour and glory and blessing. Thou wast slain and by thy blood didst ransom men for God, from every tribe and tongue and people and nation and hast made them a kingdom and priests to our God and they shall reign on earth. Even so come Lord Jesus. Amen.

FURTHER READING

Experience in Groups by W. R. Bion (Tavistock). A pioneer of group-therapy: hard work but worth it!

The Red Book of Groups by Gaie Houston (The Rochester Foundation, 8 Rochester Terrace, London W1 1984). A fun book.

Life Together by Dietrich Bonhoeffer (SCM 1954). A Christian classic.

Parable of Community by Brother Roger of Taizé (Mowbrays 1980). (The-Spirit-in-Action-Today!)

Chapter Eleven

MAKING IT HAPPEN: THE FACILITATOR'S ROLE

THIS CHAPTER IS for 'the professionals' rather than for the general reader. We are *all* called to greater understanding of ourselves and others. Many are called to become Christian listeners, serving people with sensitivity and love. Others will know themselves called to positions of ministry (lay or ordained) and find themselves praying for individuals or couples in depth.

But comparatively few seem to be called on for the 'skilled-craftsman' approach which this chapter describes. May it encourage those who are, and point the way forward for those who one day will be.

Whether you see yourself as group leader, facilitator, therapist, minister, or know a calling to such a role, this chapter is about *doing it*; about improving the skills you have and learning new ones.

You need the adroitness of a tennis coach, the patience and resilience of a midwife, and the demanding exactitude of a music teacher.

It all looks so easy when we watch someone else or read vivid accounts. Take heart, all skills can be acquired and disciplines learned. As for spiritual gifts, they only have to be *received*!

In brief this chapter will answer these questions:

What is the facilitator's inner mind-set?
What is his own process?
What is she aiming to *do*?
How does he accomplish it?

Are there necessary assumptions or is there even a philosophy behind her approaches?

My son, be attentive to my words; incline your ear to my sayings. Let them not escape from your sight; keep them within your heart. For they are life to him who finds them, and healing to all his flesh. Keep your heart with all vigilance, for from it flow the springs of life. Put away from you crooked speech and put devious talk far from you. Let your eyes look directly forward and your gaze be straight before you. Take heed to the path of your feet, then all your ways will be sure. Do not swerve to the right or to the left; turn your foot away from evil. (Prov. 4:20–7 RSV)

In other words, 'Tell it like it is!' – wisdom, surely from the writer of Proverbs, but how difficult it is to talk straight, to say what we mean and to mean what we say! For the leader of a group and the would-be helper of others, however, it is an essential place to begin. So much of our everyday conversation swerves to the right or to the left, avoids real contact, ignores real feelings; we are past masters at side-stepping the point, missing the mark, allowing the trouble to go undetected until it is too late. But the policy of 'anything for a quiet life' usually ends in explosions. Life has the habit of catching up with us, its emotional bills must be paid. Agendas must be finished, and truth will ultimately out.

Jesus said, 'The truth shall set you free.'

We know what he means but it seems so difficult to live like that. We must now explore ways of reaching personal truth, and enabling that freedom to happen.

Paul encourages us to 'speak the truth in love' and this must be the primary disposition of the facilitator or counsellor. Carl Rogers uses words like 'genuine warmth, positive regard, prizing the person for who they are and what they are.' Nobody feels ready to work until they are satisfied that the relationship between 'thee and me' feels comfortable. Part of this respectful attitude includes the knowledge that this person does really want to work, does want to find a way through their difficulty . . . to clear away the confusion of darkness and half-truth and to walk in the light. The other part of our perception of the person facing us is that he or she is unlikely to be able to do this immediately and straightforwardly. There are probably layers of resistance to be worked through, denials of feeling, repression of memories, a certain inner fragmentation and much hidden pain which will be heavily defended. Such defences we sometimes call 'blocks'. Most of us are unaware of our blocks most of the time. The facilitator's work is to help us to become aware of how we block ourselves, and once this is realised to help us to act upon the new perception. We need to know how to do what is necessary to obtain what we *really* want, given the way the world is.

It is a process of becoming 'real' and when it happens both for the person and for the group, there is a great experience of release and joy. This is the breakthrough experience, this is wholeness and revelation, this is a completed 'Gestalt'. Tim 'arrives' when he says, 'But *I* can change'. Jane 'arrives' when she says to Top-Dog, 'I'm not ever going to let you get to that size again.' Sam begins to realise that another attitude to doctors is a possibility, and Liz says, 'I can go back to those points and try again.'

When someone begins to pour out their troubles it is like a whole heap of objects on a table at a jumble sale. They need to be sorted out, sized up and price-tagged. Where on earth do we start in what appears to be such a heap of jumble? There is usually *one* thing – a person, an event, a relationship, sometimes an object or even a dream – which will give you the way in. So choose your working subject matter and agree on it. From a state of fragmentation (the person's jumbled outpouring) move towards *separation*, that is, polarisation of the opposites within the person, come to terms with both sides – this involves the kind of dialogue Tim had with his father, and Sam had with his doctors – then move towards the agreement and reconciliation that we may call 'integration'. John achieves it for a beautiful moment when he says, 'I have nothing to give you but what I am. I cannot be another person and I choose not to be another person.'

You will spot in the initial phases many stages of phoney behaviour. These are the games people play. 'I play games to keep you at arm's length and to avoid you or anybody else getting near my vulnerable hurt area. I may intellectualise continually, I may play stupid, I may play the fool or joker, I may be the diverting story-teller. I may be skilled at one-upmanship, or my games may take more sinister forms like alcoholism, crime or other addictions. I may play "psychiatry" or I may moralise and play "preacher".' Elizabeth's game was continuously to lead us on and then to withdraw, or to go off at a tangent, whilst Bob wanted to flood us with well-meaning questions and explanations. The process of becoming real will include the realisation that this particular lifestyle is not being fully myself – I am not true to who I am, what I was created to be. Therefore to some extent I am hiding and in a process of deception. I deceive you, I deceive myself.

When I turn from this and abandon games-play *I am liable to find either a desolate wilderness or a place of pressure and turmoil within.* This area Fritz Perls called 'The Implosive Layer' – it seems that everything is crowding in on me and I cannot cope. This is, after all, the reason I have been seeking escapes, avoidances, playing games. Being *me* stuck *here* is just too painful to bear. I find myself at the *impasse*, I feel I cannot move forward or back. There is a choice ahead of me, similar in kind to that which Jesus took in the Garden of Gethsemane. He could so easily have backed off and avoided the trial, arrest and all that followed.

Pushing through the stuck place may be a moment of high drama as with Jane or it may be a quiet, deliberate choice, as with Lillian. We are often so afraid of the feelings which lie through that narrow place. We fear the thought of being out of control – would I disintegrate or go mad or commit some outrage? In the safety of the group, I take the risk and move into the *explosive* layer. My memories and the real feelings attached to them are now connected up and I am given opportunities safely to express and to act out all that needs to be said and done. The new-found freedom to do this releases me into a place of expansiveness and a sense of the possession of all my faculties. The missing parts of myself have been found and reclaimed. I need to follow this working through with a time of assimilation, the reordering of my life in the light of what I now know about who I am. I can picture myself in the familiar situations of my life, but behaving differently I can choose to act on new beliefs which will determine my feelings and actions in future. I can choose to be honest. Sam's next encounter with the hospital was a far more positive experience for him. Charles's sense of poise and belonging in his peer group at home came as a joyful surprise to him!

Our responsibility as group leaders or counsellors is not necessarily to insist that this process is followed step by step and that all insights are thoroughly learned and assimilated. We are there simply to enable those who wish to work to do so, to provide them with the maximum awareness possible of their own process, and, by our encouraging presence, to assure them that the *impasse* need not have the last word: a genuinely pastoral task! With the help of others, we provide an environment in which it is safe to take risks and to encounter one's own healing and integration arising from within. To that extent we are like midwives, bringing to birth new possibilities. But, we cannot win them all. We do not *have* to win; sometimes a person's desire to remain hidden is stronger than his desire to be healed in spite of all the inconvenience and difficulty this produces in his life. So be it, the choice remains with the person working. At any stage the choice must always be there – to go on, or to turn back. Bob's resistances to insight were very high. We had to short-circuit the logical mind by using imagery. The strong pictures may help him to make his next set of connections and identify the people who caused the 'damming'. But not yet.

A good healer in this style of work is someone who trusts her hunches and intuitions, trusts her group, knows her own resources, can be tender, or tough, keeps her sense of humour and when it feels as if *she* is walking on the water keeps her eyes fixed on him who calls.

Gestalt is a shorthand German word for many of the assumptions outlined above. Like an elephant it is hard to define, but 'I know one when I see one'. The word is like, but not the same as a few English words: form, shape, whole, configuration, structure, theme. A Gestalt is a *meaningful organised whole*, which is the way most of us would like our inner life to be.

When the unfinished business of the past is completed a sense of healing and wholeness occurs in that part of our life. Christians are able to invoke the power and healing love of the Spirit of Jesus within us and in our midst, and thus have access to a spiritual dimension which is 'bigger-than-all-of-us'.

Full healing brings the Jesus of now into the experiences of the past in such a way that guilt is forgiven, bondages are broken, the captive parts released and brokenness restored to wholeness. His good news is spoken to the *heart* so that we can walk forward in newness of life.

It is in a sense a contradiction in terms to define or write about Gestalt therapy. It is concerned with an ever increasing present awareness of ourselves and our processes, both inter-personally and within. It cannot be learned from a book or a set of principles. It can be acquired as a style or an attitude by watching it work, by seeing how it is effective and then by imitating. Jesus never wrote a book, his training pro-gramme had three steps. He said to his followers in effect: 'Watch me do it' (see Mark 9:14–29), 'Now *you* do it with me here' (see Mark 6:7–11), and 'Now you go and do it on your own' (see Mark 16:15-end). These steps are vital for us too. We must watch and learn from someone. We must learn to work in a supervised situation. It is important to find a guide and mentor and to stay in touch for many years.

There are nevertheless certain disciplines to be adhered to and some tempting avenues to be avoided if we want to make our helping role accurate and incisive. The Three Ges-talt Rules form a good basis: Here and Now; I and Thou; Not Why but How.

1. Here and Now

There is a quality of immediacy about the work recorded in this book. Although I sometimes encourage people to write their story, actual case history taking has no part in this method. Discursive analysis and lengthy accounts from the past are taboo for the time being. They function as defences which remove our awareness from this room and what is happening in the present moment. Such questions as, 'What is happening now?', 'What is your present awareness?', 'What is your process?' bring us back into the present and keep the focus right *here* and right *now*.

2. I and Thou

The immediacy of what is going on between you and me in these present circumstances has to be kept always in view. It will give the key as to how this person functions in the world outside. It will open the door to the drama taking place in the interior 'house' as well.

3. Not 'Why?' but 'How?'

We need a quick way through the mental labyrinth. We short-cut all intellectualism, rationalisations, interpretations and analysis. All of these things have their place elsewhere. Very occasionally it is necessary to stop for moments of clarification and explanation, but such things are normally confined to teaching sessions at other times. When we are working, 'why-questions' are forbidden and only 'how-questions' matter. 'How do you feel at this moment?' is a more appropriate question than, 'Why do you think you have a headache?' Why-questions lead to 'because-answers' and take us down a trail of pitfalls and diversions, leading to general discussion of principles, causes and effects, all of which may be interesting, but successfully avoid working deeper into a person's place of implosion and release.

With these three principles clearly in mind you can take a firm hand in editing and redirecting the conversation. It is as if you are an instructor in a dual control car, now and again *you even take the liberty of applying the brake yourself or redirecting the steering wheel and suggesting the route ahead.*

One thing to edit is what we call *gossip*. If I start to talk *about* someone or *about* my situation, please call me to order. Ask me to address the situation directly, to talk *to* my job, *to* my wife, mother-in-law, father or sister. Put a cushion on an empty chair and insist that I talk *to* the person concerned, rather than about them. The reality I need to discover happens when I speak directly without the crooked speech which deviates and swerves to right or to left. In a word I must 'tell it like it is' and get the message straight to the person it's intended for. Such direct talk will usually connect me to the feelings associated with this person or this situation-I'm-in and the helper must encourage the expression of such feelings.

They may begin to appear little by little – an inflection, a change in facial expression, a movement of the foot, even a pause, a silence. The helper will ask me to exaggerate this, to do it again, to say it louder, even to shout. I need a good deal of help to do that which I am chronically unaccustomed to doing, i.e. feeling my feelings and expressing them clearly to the person they are intended for. My helper needs to be looking for these avoidances in my usual lifestyle. What is missing? Sometimes, for example, a whole area of my body will appear inert, dead and this will give the clue to my avoidances or repressions. (Remember Tim's lower limbs?) My helper is watching such body language. Facial expression, tones of voice, movements of arms, legs, hands and feet will all speak so much more clearly than my actual words. My choice of words is important, however, and you will help me by following the colourful phrase, the emotive word or something that I frequently repeat. You may ask me what that means to me, you may ask me to repeat it or you may tell me to go for its complete opposite and explore that.

In an extraordinary way our feelings coexist within us. Strength and weakness are not far apart, love and hate, sadness and joy. As a helper or therapist I need to be free to follow my own feelings about the way the conversation is going. Led by the Spirit, I may have a hunch, an intuition, a phrase which keeps coming to mind, I may have a perception which is quite at variance to that which I am being told verbally. For me the phrase 'Blind man's buff' came into my head twice during John's work. The word 'illegitimate' was present during part of Charles's work. I need to be free to express this, to intervene actively and to use the group to check out my new lead.

If, as the client-person, I continue to avoid and deflect my helper's suggestions, I continue to speak in an impersonal way and to resist and block my own work, he is right to confront me with what he sees. Sometimes, as with Liz in Chapter 8, a direct and somewhat exasperated confrontation can lead to the breakthrough that is needed. Other ways of helping someone who seems intractably stuck and unable to move are humour and perhaps a break for coffee, a change of approach, for example, physical approaches, acting out, or a direct prayer approach with authority over resisting spirits. In the last resort, the shock tactics of closing the work or walking out are an effective way of saying, 'Please don't waste our time any longer!' It's cruel to be kind – it's usually effective.

When a Christian group is participating in a lively way I believe it has within it all the resources for healing and change that a person needs for today. It is up to me to trust the group and to use those resources appropriately. They will check out my perceptions and add ones of their own which may be complementary. One person will be writing a verbatim script of the whole encounter. Sometimes the person working will do the rounds by asking something or stating something to each member of the group. Remember at each session the group represents the whole world. It is the stage on which the drama is taking place. It is the safety net above which I dare to walk my tightrope. It is the safe environment in which I can choose to show my weakness and hurt.

Group members can also be useful as role players in dramatic sequences. Eileen was working in a group recently, she has two artificial legs and from childhood has felt excluded. She recalled a memory of standing in a corner in the playground while the others enjoyed a game. The group could re-enact this for her, behaving like children, playing in the middle of the room, whilst she stood on the edge and re-experienced some of her early feelings. But now she had liberty to change her reaction. The 'Gestalt' did not need to remain 'fixed'. She chose to shout, *'Let me in, let me in'* and she had to shout very loudly to be heard by the playing children. Finally, the group subsided and admitted her to full membership and found her a part to play.

The woman who is afraid in the presence of men finds herself able to address the men in the group about this fear. The man with doubts and uncertainties about his own sexuality will find himself able to speak to women present about this and receive reassurance. The dominant and over-assertive person will receive straight feedback from the group in a way which ordinary life does not usually permit. Although I described the working situation as a dual-controlled car, ultimately the client-person is in charge and must always be allowed the freedom to drive on or stop the vehicle. The co-driver's or facilitator's mode is to suggest, to observe, to make clear and to offer new directions.

He or she is always looking for the opening which will provide the next avenue to move the car along. Sometimes such an avenue is provided by a dream or dream fragment, sometimes by an incident that happened today, sometimes by the person's own fantasies about the room or the group, sometimes a favourite Bible story can be used, for example, 'Who do you identify with in the parable of the Prodigal Son? Become that person and tell us how you are feeling about the situation.' Sometimes deliberately guided imagery is indicated as in the case of Bob in Chapter 4. When dreams, incidents or fantasies are used, always ask the working person to bring the encounter into the present moment, e.g. 'I am standing in this hall of mirrors. Feeling very sure of myself I move towards the nearest one and the image changes into a crocodile', etc., etc.

Every part of my dream or fantasy represents part of myself and fruitful dialogue can take place with a dream fragment just as much as with part of the body, a symptom, or with another person in order to make meaningful readjustments in my inner world. It is difficult indeed to work with the presentation of cosmic feelings like anger, worthlessness, meaninglessness, boredom, grief. It becomes easier when these are symbolised by some person, creature or object in a dream.

A further step towards reality is to change the *symbols* into the *people* in my inner world that they represent. Thus Tim in Chapter 2 began by talking about nameless fears, trepidations, anxieties, continued by symbolising these as pursuers through a forest, and ended up by speaking to, and indeed, confronting his father.

In most of the work coming out of the group in this book you will notice, time after time, turning-points when the person plucks up courage, takes a risk, moves in a direction they had not thought of before. Phrases like, 'the penny dropped', 'it dawned on me', 'I suddenly saw what I had been doing' are often used at these points. But before such disclosure situations can be reached there is often a great deal of resistance, avoidance and running away. If I become aware that this is your process it is my responsibility to *frustrate* you at every turn and bring you back to the impasse, the apparently impossible choice before you. *That point of frustration is your growing point.* It is the point of make or break. You may be like the horse that runs up to the water-jump several times before finally clearing it. It is my responsibility to keep your head in the direction of that jump and no other easier or attractive jump to right or left.

The letter from Liz following her story in Chapter 8 is ample evidence that she appreciated my being 'hard on her and tough with her' as she described it, in order finally to summon up the energy needed for the big jump.

To conclude a work period it often clarifies what has happened, both to the group and to the person working, to come back to the original circumstances with which the work began and readdress this circumstance or person. Thus, Charles in Chapter 9 was asked to do the rounds again at the end of his work time. He was able to meet each person on a very different level as a result of the experiences he had just come through. It will be up to Charles to become aware of his freedom now to choose the level he wishes to be on in any group of people. He is no longer bound by the old lies of inferiority or illegitimacy. His script-writer needs to get together with him soon after the work, to point out the things he said and had believed all his life. Together they must find ways in which to re-educate his thinking or to renew his mind. Negating what went before, affirming new freedoms he has entered and undergirding *both* with the strengthening Word of God, he will keep the territory he has won. He can expect a new richness in encountering people of every background and education, across the board. 'It all looks so easy when we watch someone else, or read vivid accounts. Take heart, all skills can be acquired and disciplines learned. As for spiritual gifts, they only have to be *received*!' So the chapter opened and it needs repeating. The skills and gifts of a counsellor are safe when received from and offered daily to the Higher Power in his or her life. I want to tell you more about this.

THE FACILITATOR'S PROGRESS: A TEACHING SUMMARY

Gestalt
'It's like an elephant, I know one when I see one!'

Gestalt Rules
1. Here and Now.
2. I and Thou.
3. Not 'Why?' but 'How?'

The Client
has the steering wheel but remember you're in a dual-control car.

Steps for Getting Somewhere
1. Finish with games, defences, avoidances.
2. Define the first area to work with.
3. Implosive layer – support, encourage, provoke, frustrate.
4. *Impasse* – move through, help person do or say the difficult thing.
5. Explosive layer – risk those real feelings, tell it like it is.
6. Renewing-the-Mind (see below).
7. Assimilate new freedoms into life.

Checklist for Renewing-the-Mind
1. Own the real feeling coming up (Mine!).
2. Negate the negative scripts.
3. Repent for having believed them so firmly for so long.
4. Posit (affirm) new positive faith-judgements.
5. Discover that God's Word confirms your decision.

Discipling
Jesus taught them thus:
1. Watch me do it.
2. Do it alongside me.
3. Now go and do it on your own.
Lastly: no gossip! (Talk *to*; not *about*)

BRINGING IT HOME

1. Turn the sound off in a TV play, interview or news programme. Read the non–verbal messages and body language.
2. 'I am responsible for my failures and weaknesses. I may actually *prefer* sickness to health. There is a hidden payoff.' How does such an approach fit in with your attitude to your aches and pains, or that difficult relationship, or that besetting sin?
3. 'The art of living is based on rhythm, on give and take, ebb and flow, light and dark, life and death. By accept-

ance of all the aspects of life – good and bad, right and wrong, yours and mine – the static, defended life, which is what we are cursed with, is converted into a dance, the dance of life. The real function of the dance is metamorphosis', Henry Miller.

Jesus has been called 'the Lord of the Dance'. How do we manage to stop ourselves 'dancing' (i.e. changing too much or too quickly)?

SCRIPTURE

Isaiah 42:5–9 The Servant of the Lord (NIV) (Facilitators-of-change, take note!)

> *This is what God the Lord says –*
> *he who created the heavens and stretched them out,*
> *who spread out the earth and all that comes out of it,*
> *who gives breath to its people,*
> *and life to those who walk on it;*
> *'I the Lord have called you in righteousness;*
> *I will take hold of your hand.*
> *I will keep you and will make you*
> *to be a covenant for the people*
> *and a light for the Gentiles,*
> *to open eyes that are blind,*
> *to free captives from prison*
> *and to release from the dungeon*
> *those who sit in darkness.*
>
> *I am the Lord, that is my name!*
> *I will not give my glory to another*
> *or my praise to idols.*
> *See, the former things have taken place,*
> *and new things I declare;*
> *before they spring into being*
> *I announce them to you.'*

PRAYER

Help us, Lord, to see our commission as coming from
you. May we hear the new things you want to declare.
May we know you as Liberator . . . as Lord of the Dance.
May we celebrate the whole of it. Amen.

FURTHER READING

Gestalt Therapy Verbatim by Fritz Perls (Real People Press
1981). Selected material from audio-tapes made at weekend seminars conducted by Perls at Esalen Institute, Big
Sur, California, in the late sixties. His introductory 'Talk'
sets out the method and philosophy of 'Gestalt'. These are
the title deeds!

Roots and Shoots by Roger Hurding (Hodder 1986): esp.
Chapter 9 'The New Therapies'. Hurding offers a balanced
critique of some of the influential newer schools of
thought. He sets them against their wider historical background and compares and contrasts their world-view with
that of the Bible. He offers a salutary warning against
the idolatry of 'extreme subjectivism and the rejection of
absolutes'.

The Relative-Sized Red Book of Gestalt by Gaie Houston (The
Rochester Foundation, 8 Rochester Terrace, London NW1
9JN, 1984). A book for fun: for simple beginnings: more
than forty exercises for small groups.

Chapter Twelve

YOUR STRENGTH IN MY WEAKNESS: A WAY OF HEALING

IF I WERE the sort of therapist described in the last chapter, always alert, sensitive, warm, congruent, confrontational, then I would certainly run the risk of becoming messianic! There would be no shortage of good friends to prick the bubble. To keep us humble there are always failures – people who remain stuck or antagonised, or who bring us face to face with our own inadequacy. The Christian counsellor has to stay dependent on God. After all it is *his healing work* that we are describing – not some kind of personal charisma or group-chemistry with magic formulae.

It is doubly necessary then, for the healer to *'abide in the vine'*, which is Christ (John 15:4, 5). He or she must ponder and emulate *his* qualities, meditate on the way *he* did it and, above all, pray his Spirit into every situation. 'Your strength in my weakness' is the correct assessment of every achievement recorded in this book. It is why such work can be called *'Christian* Growth and Gestalt'.

How did Jesus go about his work? Centuries before, the prophet Isaiah was able to define quite sharply the qualities the promised Messiah would have.

> *Here is my servant whom I uphold,*
> *my chosen one in whom I delight;*
> *I will put my Spirit on him*

> *and he will bring justice to the nations.*
> *He will not shout or cry out*
> *or raise his voice in the streets.*
> *A bruised reed he will not break,*
> *and a smouldering wick he will not snuff out.*
> *In faithfulness he will bring forth justice;*
> *he will not falter or be discouraged*
> *till he establishes justice on earth . . .*
> *I, the Lord, have called you in righteousness;*
> *I will take hold of your hand.*
> *I will keep you and make you to be*
> *a covenant for the people*
> *and a light for the Gentiles,*
> *to open eyes that are blind,*
> *to free captives from prison*
> *and to release from the dungeon*
> *those who sit in darkness.*
> (Isa. 42:1–4a, 6b, 7 NIV)

Thus the promised Messiah, or Saviour, was to have this combination of tough and tender attributes. He would know when to challenge, he would know when to protect and encourage, he would know how to declare God's truth with all the conviction of light dawning in dark places.

Here he is meeting some of the people of his day and then, by extension, some of our contemporaries – the people of our group. Jesus is prepared to take risks . . . it was unthinkable for a rabbi to be seen talking to a woman, and to a Samaritan one at that. As we follow the dialogue in John 4 it is clear that he values her, he esteems her fully as a person, with a personal story and personal needs. He asks her to meet his need for a drink, and then talks about the kind of thirst he knows *she* has. One of *her* needs seemed to be secrecy: he meets it by using his gift of knowledge about her past. Another defence was deflection, 'Let's talk about worship rather than my difficulties.' Jesus follows the flow but brings her back to the present, the here-and-now, and I-and-thou (I who speak to you am he!). When she asks in effect, 'Why *should* we worship in Jerusalem?' Jesus sidesteps, answering instead the *How* question which underlay the old controversy. (*'God is spirit and his worshippers must worship in spirit and in truth.'*) Jesus' own immediacy and *contact* with people predated the Gestalt rules by two thousand years. They authenticate them vividly. Jesus finished another encounter with a woman (taken in adultery, John 8:4), *'Neither do I condemn you. Go now and leave your life of sin'* (NIV). We might have anticipated a response of mercy and tenderness in his meeting with Elizabeth in Chapter 8.

He is prepared to confront quickly, even sharply. The rich young man in Matthew 19:16–22 was sincere and respectful. Jesus received his persistent questions and answered them in orthodox fashion. But he knew that each one was a 'hook'. Perhaps the young man was expecting to elicit reassurance from Jesus – 'You're doing fine, you need nothing more' – but his deeper self, dissatisfied and knowing that his wealth was bringing more worry than happiness, blurted out, 'What do I still lack?' Jesus knew his fixation on material security and addressed it directly, in fact he goes for its opposite polarity – abandoned generosity! – '. . . *If you want to be perfect, go, sell your possessions and give to the poor and you will have treasure in heaven. Then come, follow me.'* (What would Jesus say to John in Chapter 5?)

The offer is refused, another near miss. The Gospel story does not record whether a second chance came the young man's way. Another chance *does* seem to have come the way of Nicodemus. We first meet him coming to Jesus by night in John 3, prepared for theological debate. Jesus introduces him to a new and revolutionary concept – the new birth; an experience which will turn his carefully balanced doctrines upside-down. In verses 16 and 17 we find the core-explanation of Jesus' whole life and death. We find, too, the motivating belief system of the Christian listener and helper. No one is really helped until his or her fundamental belief system is changed. *'For God so loved the world that he gave his one and only Son that whoever believes in him shall not perish but have eternal life. For God did not send his Son into the world to condemn the world but to save the world through him'* (NIV). It was an impossible message for most of the lawyers and rulers to accept. (Jane of Chapter 3 is still struggling with it. All the critical parental figures of our own personal attic have to come to terms with it. Not condemn? Unthinkable! . . . It's what we're here for!)

'*Later, Joseph of Arimathea asked Pilate for the body of Jesus . . . He was accompanied by Nicodemus, the man who earlier had visited Jesus by night. Nicodemus brought a mixture of myrrh and aloes, about seventy-five pounds* . . . ' John 19:38–9 (NIV). Nicodemus was prepared for the gospel of grace – for the Renewal of his (theological) Mind!

Elizabeth, Jane and John, Tim, Bob, Lillian, Sam and Charles . . . we have followed the fortunes of eight people in this book, nine if I include myself. Not one would claim that their healing is complete, but they are walking forward, making progress. They are on a way of healing and well aware of the milestones they have passed. Sometimes, they would all agree, the Lord comes very close and speaks directly to their condition. This clear speaking has the power of revelation and calls for response; either I must believe it and that will mean change, or I must plod on as before and not allow those words into my heart. In our final cameo I envisage all members of the group sharing in an episode which has particular poignancy for me.

Two friends are trudging home after the Crucifixion. Heavy, sad, desolate, they were on the way to Emmaus. Their pace was slow, their heads down, with shoulders drooping. 'Jesus is dead', they firmly believe, 'our hopes are dashed, the last three years wasted. Everything he stood for and we believed in is destroyed. We saw it happen.' The stranger draws alongside; they hardly bother to look up. He doesn't seem to know what's been happening. '*What things?*' he asks, and they pour out the whole sorry story. He says to them. "*O foolish men, and slow of heart to believe all that the prophets have spoken! Was it not necessary that the Christ should suffer these things and enter into his glory?*" *And beginning with Moses and all the prophets, he interpreted to them in all the scriptures the things concerning himself*' (Luke 24:25–7 RSV).

I see in this brief encounter a beautiful vignette of inner healing. Jesus draws near, walks alongside, patiently hears them out, then speaks directly to their condition – not much for their comfort or consolation, but plenty to jolt and challenge them. In today's venacular, 'You idiots, what did you expect?' As he continues to confront, to explain, to restore their faith, they feel their icy hearts melting, '*Did not our hearts burn within us?*' Finally at Emmaus when he breaks the bread they recognise him. 'God is with us again.' Then they had energy to go and tell. The group in Jerusalem knew already. In a word, healing took place as soon as their beliefs about themselves and their situation changed. Their feelings altered and then their lifestyle was radically affected. I see it as a glorious example of a completed Gestalt – a need is expressed, resources draw near, supply meets demand, need is fully met. 'We're on our way again. What's next?'

In my mind's eye I see the people we've met in these chapters trudging on the Emmaus road. Jesus draws near, speaks to their condition and waits for their response.

TIM (the man who ran away) 'Tim, take heart. Stand on your feet. Turn and face those people again and again, I will give you a Spirit of Power and Love and of Sound Mind.'

JANE (the woman in the dock) 'Jane, I do not condemn you, I've already put an end to that harsh voice within you. Now listen to me instead! Let me be peacemaker in your civil war.'

BOB (the man who wouldn't listen) 'Bob, from now on it's Robert. *I'll* ask the questions, *I'll* do the explaining, sit up and take notice, look and listen, watch and pray. I want to show you the map of your river, right back to source.'

JOHN (the Michelin man) 'John, turn around, tear up your colour supplement, you are of more value than many hi-fis. You're right, it's the whole bit, body, mind and spirit. Give all you are and come – follow me.'

LILLIAN (the girl who couldn't belong) 'Lillian, so now you know. When they forsook you I took you up. I have called you by name, you are mine, I will not let you go. I love you.'

SAM (the man who sat on a volcano) 'Sam, your spirit is not confined to a wheelchair. With me you will be an overcomer and lead many along this way. Turn your anger to my praise; remember those tables in the temple – they were for turning!'

ELIZABETH (the girl who played hide-and-seek) 'Elizabeth, in my eyes you're okay. I want to turn your trudge into a dance, your mourning into joy. Get up, it's *you* we're waiting for, no more hiding, no more teasing, you're okay and I love you.'

CHARLES (the man who felt stupid) 'Charles, they pushed me to the bottom of the pile too. Take your legitimate place with me, with my people. Receive my authority to do the things I do, I commission you now.'

THE AUTHOR (wondering which way next) 'Ian, a point of arrival becomes a point of departure. My way of healing has become clear to you, pass it on but don't think you have got it all, you've only just begun!'

It is true. I often feel right at the beginning of learning to help and heal. There are so many good books to read and digest! I comfort myself by remembering that 'there is nothing so practical as a good theory'. I have kept the theorising to a deliberate minimum because I believe God wants to manifest himself in practice; in encounter; in decisive change. We may prefer thinking: God prefers action!

I know some Christians will say, 'Where is all this in Scripture?' I have produced biblical material with each chapter for reflection and illumination for those with eyes to see and ears to hear. I know other people who will cry, 'Why bring God into all this at all?' I respond that Christians do not need to *bring* God in, he's there already. We do, however, want to give credit where credit is due. God seems to insist on 'getting in on the act' as if he had a proprietary right. We believe he has. He has particular ways and means for us to learn and powers to put at our disposal. I believe these things are more than just another language to describe phenomena. They certainly are that *at least* (every approach needs its own coinage). I believe they are more a way of being in the world, a way of seeing in the world, a way of liberating the complete potential of human life – physical, emotional and spiritual. God, dwelling in light unapproachable and yet made manifest in Jesus Christ, is the final completion of our process, the final meeting of all our needs, the Gestalt of gestalts!

God is eager for the Here and Now experience, for the I-Thou relationship. God seeks us out, he calls, initiates, provokes and answers, and, like a persistent lover who will not take 'No' for an answer, he changes us. He is the great catalyst in the chemistry of life and growth. Jane referred to her session in a letter as a 'burning-bush experience'. That would be echoed by all our travellers; we all share Moses' amazement and acute discomfort when the ordinary and obvious are alight with new meaning and significance, and when change is relentlessly called for. God seems to be saying, 'It's my world and I want it back; *you're* my person and I want you back.' He wants the dark continent, our own 'unexplored interior' to be fully and completely evangelised!

Jesus had the gift of putting this profound truth into simple sayings. Here are a dozen signposts which point up the healing way for me (unless otherwise stated, all from New RSV):

'*Repent and believe the good news*' (Mark 1:15). Why his continuous emphasis on a turning to new *belief*? Because that is the heart of the matter, it is our 'self talk', our innermost scripts which condition our outlook and lives. In every life changed to his way there are the necessary times of repentance to be negotiated, in the sense of turning away from false personal beliefs. Each turning-point will lead to an appropriation of new truth. As one group member wrote, 'I used to think that the cost was in being willing to go through all the pain and hurt again, but now I think that it's being willing to change or even be changed.'

Jesus is evidently more concerned with the '*how*' of life. He tells us how to turn, how to pray, then how to choose, feel, act, live. The 'why-questions' can wait.

'*The kingdom of heaven is within you*' (Luke 17:21 TEV) – not halfway round the world, in Nepal or California (no disrespect intended to those beautiful places), nor in libraries, films or videos. God's sovereignty, his kingly rule has to be found first and foremost within those personal experiences, memories, hurts and fears that make up 'me', or it will be found nowhere else. *Your* healing is within *you, mine* within *me.* Lillian discovered him this way.

The New RSV has for the above verse: '*The kingdom of God is among you*' (in your midst) – it is found in relationship, in interaction, it is a group experience. It is for those who are willing to submit to his rule and to each other and to travel together, it is a body event. God's kingly rule is expressed in an 'I/Thou' relationship and not in a theory or a philosophy. The call is always to a form of shared life, a group, a community, a communion, a church.

'*The kingdom is at hand*' (Mark 1:15 RSV) – as near as my hand, a hand's touch away. Kingdom life happens when we make contact, when we are really in touch with our inner selves, our neighbours, our environment, and with God. It is a here and now event, reality breaks through with a quality of surprise so often in healing work. The breakthrough of the Kingdom of God is discernible in one of the dialogues quoted here. Once John relinquished control, it was all there, *at hand*! (Chapter 5.)

'*The Son of Man came to seek out and save the lost*' (Luke 19:10) – three of Jesus' most vivid parables, in Luke 15, concern a lost sheep, a lost coin and a lost son. If there is something missing, if you have overlooked or even dismissed something (or someone), you will have no rest until you find it or until the family circle is complete. If part of yourself is being neglected you have no peace of mind or body until you have begun the search. Tim needed to find his feet in Chapter 2, and Lillian her identity in Chapter 6. If you have banished a person to outer darkness then look out too. He or she is still there waiting for acknowledgement and peace.

'*Come to terms quickly with your accuser while you are on the way to court with him*' (Matt. 5:25) – the result of leaving enmities festering, affairs unsettled, or grievances unresolved, is that we ourselves are jailed for debt and not let out until we pay the last farthing. So pay attention to unfinished business, it has a habit of catching up with you.

Even more demanding: '*Love your enemies*' (Matt. 5:44) – Jesus knew the power of hate and resentment to keep us imprisoned within. This 'impossible demand' was in fact very good liberation-theology. Through the impasse (the things I dare not say or express for fear of outrage, murder or destruction), through and onward, we reach a place of calm where reconciliation and even love become possibilities. In Judaism, with its respect for the Law, 'Top Dog' was as active to promote inhibition and prohibition in Jesus' day as in ours. Sam and Jane would say 'Amen'.

'Woe also to you lawyers! For you load people with burdens hard to bear, and you yourselves do not lift a finger to ease them' (Luke 11:46) – when Jesus came on the scene a new dimension was present; what else to call it but 'the grace of God'? He said to the woman caught in the act of adultery, *'Neither do I condemn you, go your way and from now on, do not sin again'* (John 8:11). No wonder Paul declared, *'Christ, the end of the Law'* (Romans 10:4). The personal inner accuser and judge, ours as well as Jane's, needs to hear his Word.

In respect of the 'Under-Dog', the hidden, wingeing child of the past: *'Let the little children come to me and do not stop them, for it is to such as these that the Kingdom of God belongs'* (Luke 18:16). He says we can only enter as 'little children', so it is not only advisable, but *essential* to be getting to know and love those parts of me in the cellar. Welcome back little lost ones! Charles has his arm round his own 'little lad' (Chapter 9).

'Render to Caesar the things that are Caesar's and to God the things that are God's' (Luke 20:25 RSV) – but how much of my life is occupied in getting and spending and how little with the inner growth and reaching out which Jesus calls 'the things that are God's'? When I get my inner priorities right I can be sure it will affect my attitude to Caesar as well. John knows the meaning of that saying – from the inside now! (Chapter 5.)

'Follow me, and let the dead bury their own dead' (Matt. 8:22) – there's an urgency about his challenge, there may not be a second chance. In group work, as in life, you have to get on with it or miss your chance and go away unsatisfied.

Jesus also said, *'You will receive power when the Holy Spirit has come upon you'* (Acts 1:8) – I'm glad he promised us this.

For by my own, unaided efforts (agree with all his sayings as I might), I could never live up to them.

Our title deeds in this work have to be from Isaiah 61. Jesus chose these words to begin his ministry.

> *The Spirit of the Lord God is upon me,*
> *because the Lord has anointed me*
> *to bring good tidings to the afflicted;*
> *he has sent me to bind up the brokenhearted,*
> *to proclaim liberty to the captives,*
> *and the opening of the prison to those who are bound;*
> *to proclaim the year of the Lord's favour,*
> *and the day of vengeance of our God;*
> *to comfort all who mourn;*
> *to grant to those who mourn in Zion –*
> *to give them a garland instead of ashes,*
> *the oil of gladness instead of mourning,*
> *the mantle of praise instead of a faint spirit;*
> *that they may be called oaks of righteousness,*
> *the planting of the Lord, that he may be glorified.*
> *They shall build up the ancient ruins,*
> *they shall raise up the former devastations,*
> *they shall repair the ruined cities,*
> *the devastations of many generations.* (RSV)

Ancient ruins and devastations are an accurate description of the bleakness of the inner landscape of many lives. Only the Spirit of the Lord can make them flourish and *'blossom like the rose'* (Isa. 35:1 AV).

Woven into the tapestry of people's accounts of healing you will read things like, 'We rested him in the Spirit, we received a prophetic word, a word of knowledge, a healing touch. I received the laying on of hands with prayer and anointing with oil. I asked for absolution and cutting free, I had a discernment. He needed deliverance ministry, the expulsion of demons. She had a picture and it gave the key. They sang in tongues. I was filled with the Spirit.' In all these signs or sacraments the Holy Spirit comes. He does not invade, he responds to invitations. His movement is always gracious, he will not push, or force his way in. It is more like an easing of the way through the 'stuck place', a lubrication of the rusty works. Even prayer-book liturgies have their place: I have used the Burial Office to re-enact a funeral for someone who had lost her gift of 'good grief'. Our conference weeks always ended on a rejoicing note with a service of Holy Communion. It spelt out in every prayer and Scripture what the course had been about and pointed the way ahead. In praise and worship, God was enthroned among us, we became aware of our heavenly citizenship and the new creation going on.

We often began by singing,

> Let Me have My way among you,
> do not strive, do not strive.
> Let Me have My way among you,
> do not strive, do not strive.
> For Mine is the power and the glory,
> for ever and ever the same.
> Let Me have My way among you,
> do not strive, do not strive.

We often ended by singing,

O Lord, you've done great things, I will praise you,
I will extol you and magnify your Name.
O Lord, you've done great things and I will praise you,
I will extol you and magnify your Name.
I will sing praises unto you and remember your goodness,
My past is forgiven and now I have life.
You crown me with steadfast love and tender mercy.
I'll do your will and bless you, O Lord.

Gaie Houston ends her *Relative-Sized Red Book of Gestalt* with a picture of seven pin men building a house. At the foot of the page are the words 'The beginning'. So be it for you, may your journey be nourished, sustained and encouraged by what you have read. May finishing this book mark a new beginning on your road ahead.

'The peace of God which passes all understanding, keep your hearts and minds in the knowledge and love of God, and of his Son Jesus Christ our Lord. Amen.'

FURTHER READING

The Christian Healing Ministry by Morris Maddocks (SPCK
1981). A comprehensive and scholarly account of the healing ministry of Jesus and the story of his healing ministry
vested in (but sometimes neglected by) the church. See
esp. Chapter 12 Healing for Society. (The mood and message of this book ripple out!)

Appendix 1

PLEASE HEAR WHAT I'M NOT SAYING

Don't be fooled by me, Don't be fooled by the face I wear.
For I wear a mask, I wear a thousand masks that I'm afraid
  to take off and none of them are me.
Pretending is an art that's second nature with me, but don't
  be fooled, for God's sake don't be fooled.
I give you the impression that I'm secure, that all is sunny
  and
    unruffled with me, within as well as without
    that confidence is my name and coolness my game,
    that the water's calm and I'm in command
    and that I need no one
But don't believe me
PLEASE!
My surface may seem smooth, but my surface is my mask
My ever-varying and ever concealing mask.
Beneath lies no smugness, no complacence,
Beneath dwells the real me in confusion, in fear, in
  aloneness.
But I hide this.
I don't want anybody to know it.
I panic at the thought of my weakness and fear being
  exposed.
That's why I frantically create a mask to hide behind,
A nonchalant, sophisticated facade, to help me pretend,
to shield me from the glance that knows.
But such a glance is precisely my salvation, my only
  salvation.
And I know it.

That is if it's followed by acceptance, if it's followed by
   love.
It's the only thing that can liberate me, from myself,
from my own self-built prison walls,
from the barriers that I so painstakingly erect.
It's the only thing that will assure me of what I can't assure
   myself – that I'm really worth something.
But I don't tell you this. (I don't dare.) I'm afraid to,
I'm afraid you'll think less of me, that you'll laugh,
   and your laugh would kill me.
I'm afraid that deep-down I'm nothing, that I'm just no
   good and that you will see this and reject me.
So I play my game, my desperate pretending game with a
   facade of
   assurance without, and a trembling child within,
   and so begins the parade of masks
   and my life becomes a front.
I idly chatter to you in suave tones of surface talk.
I tell you everything that's really nothing,
And nothing of what's everything, of what's crying within
   me.
So when I'm going through my routine do not be fooled
   by what I'm saying.
Please listen carefully and try to hear what I'm not saying,
What I'd like to be able to say, what for survival I need to
   say,
But what I can't say.
I dislike hiding. Honestly.
I dislike the superficial game I'm playing, the superficial
   phony game
I'd really like to be genuine and spontaneous, and me, but
   you've got to help me, I've got to hold your hand,
Even when that's the last thing I seem to want, or need.
Only you can wipe away from my eyes the blank stare of
   the breathing dead.
Only you can call me into aliveness.
Each time you're kind, and gentle, and encouraging,
Each time you try to understand because you really care,

My heart begins to grow wings, very small wings, very
  feeble wings, but wings.
With your sensitivity and sympathy, and your power of
  understanding,
You can breathe life into me. I want you to know that.
I want you to know how important you are to me, how
  you can be a
Creator of the person that is me if you choose to.
Please choose to.
You alone can break down the wall behind which I tremble.
You alone can remove my mask.
You alone can release me from my shadow-world of panic
  and uncertainty
From my lonely prison. So do not pass me by. Please do
  not pass me by.
It will not be easy for you.
A long conviction of worthlessness builds strong walls.
The nearer you approach to me, the blinder I may strike
  back.
It's irrational, but despite what books say about man, I am
  irrational.
I fight against the very thing that I cry out for. But I am
  told
  that love is stronger than walls, and in this lies my hope.
My only hope.
Please try to beat down these walls with firm hands, but
  with gentle hands,
For a child is very sensitive.
Who am I, you may wonder?
I am someone you know very well.
For I am every man you meet and
I am every woman you meet.

Written by a member of the community at Chula Vista,
California.

Appendix 2

WHAT EXACTLY IS ... GESTALT?

In Chapter 11 I give a working model of Gestalt therapy. This is the process which the therapist has in mind when 'working' with a client. Throughout the book I enumerate attitudes or techniques which have a 'Gestalt' flavour or ethos. The book deals with 'Christian Gestalt' because it is permeated by Scripture and saturated by the Spirit of God. I have thus baptised a useful tool-kit and caused it to serve the Kingdom.

Gestalt had German origins. In 1912 three young psychologists who were particularly interested in human perception joined forces to found the Berlin Gestalt School. An individual, they proposed, should be understood as 'a meaningful whole'. Their work was chiefly concerned with learning-theory. Gestalt therapy pioneered by Frederick (Fritz) and Laura Perls includes this original holism, as well as looking to psychoanalytic, humanistic, existential and transpersonal influences. To quote Roger Hurding (*Roots and Shoots*, Hodder 1986), 'Perls, 1893–1970, ... whose flavour has been described as lusty, energetic, colloquial and charismatic, was a key figure in the Human Potential Movement based at Esalen in California in the 1960s. He admits that there is no precise English word to translate the word "Gestalt", but suggests that "configuration, structure, theme, structural relationship, or meaningful organised whole" most closely approximate.'

Gestalt is concerned with increasing awareness of ourselves, as *whole* beings (Body/Soul/Spirit). It is a way of de-conditioning, de-controlling our bodies. If I want to enjoy my life I need to know what feels good or bad for me and find ways of maximising the good and minimising the bad. Gestalt is about making 'wholes' of the unfinished bits of my life. Life is perceived as the emergence of one need-to-be-met after another. 'Work' or therapy helps to contact, recognise and to complete the 'unfinished-business' of my life.

Christian Gestalt includes spiritual needs and the realities of God's revelation. At this point it parts company with the secular remit of its originators, and with those practitioners who prefer to keep their faith and their work in separate compartments. Gestalt, then, is a tool, a way of seeing, a wholeness of perception, a method of personal growth, a grasping of hoped-for possibilities, like faith itself . . . *'the assurance of things hoped for, the certainty of things unseen'* (Heb. 11:1, 2). It includes the elements of birth, struggle, frustration, release, death, resurrection . . . all human life is here – in its pathos and its glory. His strength is found in our weakness!

GLOSSARY

Acting-out: Allowing feelings and impulses their full expression in the safe context of a therapy-group.

Anointing: This is a sacrament of the church using olive oil. It is an 'outward and visible sign of an inward and spiritual grace' – usually healing or reconciliation; sometimes used at Baptism . . . also at Coronations!

Blocks, blocking: Preventing access to feelings or repressed memories. This may take physical forms like shallow breathing, or tightening muscles (e.g. diaphragm) or conversational forms like diversion tactics, avoidances, etc.

Body language: Perls says the body always 'speaks' more truthfully than the words. Posture, facial expression, hand or foot movements, tone of voice, active/inert areas – even tics, itches or involuntary spasms all give direct clues to a person's inner process.

Closure: A sense that a worthwhile piece of work has been accomplished.

Confrontation: A direct statement of a truth that may be uncomfortable or difficult to handle.

Deliverance: Authoritative prayer to release someone from demonic oppression, (as in 'deliver us from evil').

Empathy: The ability to stand 'in another person's shoes'. Sensitive, supportive listening with ability to recognise and respond to feeling content.

Encounter: Shorthand for 'the dynamics of face-to-face meeting, usually in groups convened for the purpose of studying and learning from human behaviour in the here-and-now life of the group'.

Encounter-bat: A sponge-rubber weapon, the use of which can act-out conflicts in the group or in a person's own inner 'house' with safety and efficiency. I have used truncheon-like sticks or broom handles equally effectively.

Evaluation-form: Method of feedback when group life is over. It usually asks about best/worst part of the experience, assessment of the leadership style, suggestions for improvement and long-term effects felt.

Games-playing: Term introduced by Eric Berne (*Games People*

Play). A style of living and relating which avoids real contact or meeting with others.

Gestalt: See Appendix 2 and Chapter 11. Unfinished Gestalt: a need not fully met, an agenda not attended to (e.g. grief-work not done years after the loss of a loved one). Fixed Gestalt: this usually implies an unsatisfactory conclusion to a process which keeps on recurring (e.g. I always get drunk at parties or I can never receive a compliment).

'Gossip': In Gestalt: talking *about* someone or something instead of addressing him/her/it directly.

Head-trip: Explaining, filling in the background, giving opinions, ideas, history (or case-history), analysis, interpretation. It avoids the three Gestalt essentials – here and now, I and thou, not why? but how?

Impasse: The place where a person is stuck.

Inner-healing: The healing of emotional hurts of the past or present.

Introjection: The way in which we 'swallow whole' a person, persons or a system from outside with all their injunctions, demands and expectations.

New RSV: The New Revised Standard Version of the Bible, published by Nelson, 1989.

NIV: New International Version published by Hodder and Stoughton, 1979.

Polarisation: Iron filings may be haphazardly scattered but when a magnet is put close they form a pattern around one pole or the other. Similarly our scattered feelings and thoughts will separate out into strongly contrasting positives and negatives enabling choices to be made or compromises arranged.

Prayer-counselling: brings a person's life in all its phases, and all its relationships into the presence of Christ for his healing, reconciling touch. Also called Healing of the Memories, Faith-imagination therapy, Soul-Healing. May be used for single episodes or consecutively for a whole life-story.

Primal integration (primal work/therapy): involves regression to conception, intra-uterine life and perinatal events. Also called Re-birthing.

Projection: The mechanism by which a person's own problem is seen quite clearly to be 'out there' in someone else. 'First sort out the log in your own eye and then you will see clearly to remove the speck in someone else's', was Jesus' comment on this common event.

Process: An involuntary, semi-conscious programme or routine by which inner life is sustained – for better or for worse. A successful 'process' ensures that needs are met, messages get home, missions are accomplished. An unsuccessful one produces frustration, deadlock, emptiness and a feeling of hopelessness or futility.

Regression: Living through experiences of the past recovering emotional content and decisions made. Especially applies to birth, infancy, childhood and teen-age years.

Re-negotiate: Rearrange the agreement or 'contract' by which the process takes place. Make some significant changes in the inner-drama so that 'impasses' may be passed through.

Renewing the Mind: Cf. Romans 12:2. Decisive changes in a person's fundamental belief system about themselves, other people, the world and God. See Four Steps pp. 118–19 and Chapter 11.

Resting in the Spirit: see explanation in Chapter 5, pp. 54–5.

Role-play: Playing the different parts in turn in one's own life-drama.

RSV: Revised Standard Version.

Scripts: (i) The full verbatim account of someone's work, taken down during the session or from a tape.

(ii) The phrases which have power to drive or restrain, to encourage or to put down. They come from deep within because they have been introjected early in life.

'Scripty phrases' sound like this: 'I can never win' 'I always make a mess of it' 'You can't trust anyone' 'I wish I'd never been born', etc. There are also positive ones which are less likely to need changing.

Self-talk: This refers to mini-scripts with which we are constantly encouraging or condemning ourselves all day long at a subconscious level.

Soul-healing: See 'Prayer-counselling'.

Speaking in tongues: (See 1 Cor. 12:10.) A prayer-language – Greek *glossolalia* – used in worship or in private devotions. Also available for use in ministries of healing and deliverance.

Spiritual gifts: See 1 Corinthians 12:1–11 for the definitive list. They are as available and operative for ministry today as they were in the early church.

Supervision: The submission of one's work and ministry to a mentor or guide. He or she gives benefit of experience, demonstrates skills, restrains or encourages. We all need (but do not always want) accountability!

Synthesis: The final outcome when two opposites (thesis and antithesis) have become reconciled.

Tongues: Usually the first spiritual gift to be manifested. A personal praise and prayer language – sometimes for ministry to groups.

Top Dog/Under-Dog: See Chapter 3. The two elements of our inner conflict – separated, polarised and given fun-names to make them user-friendly.

Transactional Analysis: A very clear teaching modelling what goes on between people and within people in terms of Parent, Adult, Child ego-states.

Visualisation: The right hemisphere of the brain produces dreams, pictures, visions. Profitable for work as they provide greater accuracy and truth than words or concepts.

Guided-visualisation can steer client into new possibilities, or reinforce prayer counselling (e.g. see Jesus in that situation with you).

Wholeness through Christ: An inter-denominational organisation in the UK specialising in training for the ministry of prayer-counselling.

Word of knowledge: another 'spiritual gift' (1 Cor. 12:8). An insight, discernment or 'hunch' which proves to be true. The Holy Spirit 'informs' inwardly without a word being spoken about the subject.

'Work':   In Gestalt and other counselling usage, to work means to draw attention to one's need in such a way as to move through to a more comfortable, resolved or 'whole' sense of your personal being with the help of a facilitator, therapist and/or supportive group. See Chapters 1 and 11 for fuller detail.

COUNSELLING AND HEALING AGENCIES

Where possible I have tried to give an indication of the style of approach of the agencies.

Acorn Christian Healing Trust (Bishop Morris Maddocks): Whitehill Chase, High Street, Bordon, Hants GU35 0AP.
Mainstream Christian healing approach.

British Association of Counselling (a national association for those working as counsellors): 37a Sheep Street, Rugby, Warwickshire CV21 3EX.

Caring Professions Concern: King's Centre, High Street, Aldershot, Hants GU11 1DH (conferences and local groups for members of the caring professions).
Charismatic emphasis.

Central School of Counselling and Therapy (has premises in fifteen cities in the UK):
Certificate in Counselling (AEB).
Professional Training in Counselling.
Students may be currently counselling, or using the skills, new to the subject or exploring an interest. Two courses are available – one based on theory and the other on skills. Completion of both comprises the Combined Certificate in Counselling (AEB), the entry requirement for the Diploma (AEB) programme. October or January entry.
The Centre for the Advancement of Counselling (CAC), externally validated and nationally recognised.
For further information: Registrar, Centre House, 56b Hale Lane, London NW7 3PR (081 906 4833).

The Christian Fellowship of Healing (Scotland): Holy Corner Church Centre, 15 Morningside Road, Edinburgh EH10 4DP.
Broad spectrum approach to healing.

Christian Listeners: Whitehill Chase, High Street, Bordon, Hants GU35 0AP (day workshops or church-based groups offering training in listening skills, part of the Acorn Trust).

The Church Army Counselling Centres: Independents Road, Blackheath, London SE3 9LG.

Church of England Board of Education: (contact Diocesan Education Officer).

Clinical Theology Seminars: Information from St Mary's House, Church Westcote, Oxford OX7 6SF.
Interface between mental-health professions and the gospel.

Counselling Institutes: Crusade for World Revival (Selwyn Hughes), Waverley Abbey House, Waverley Lane, Farnham, Surrey GU9 8EP.
Evangelical Christian emphasis.

Cruse: bereavement counselling (see local phone directory or CAB).

Ellel Grange: Galgate, Lancaster LA2 0HN (a centre for Christian healing, counselling and training, specialising in Deliverance ministries).
Charismatic emphasis.

Institute of Psychosexual Medicine: 11 Chandos Street, Cavendish Square, London W1.

Introduction to Pastoral Counselling: Extension Studies Department, St John's College, Bramcote, Nottingham NG9 3DS. (A course including correspondence units, introductory weekend and summer school.) Also Diploma Course jointly sponsored with Nottingham University.

The Lincoln Clinic: (full-time and part-time courses in counselling). The Lincoln Institute and Clinic for Psychotherapy, Lincoln Tower, Westminster Bridge Road, London SE1 (071 261 9236).

The London Healing Mission: 20 Dawson Place, London W2 4TL.
Charismatic emphasis.

Marriage Encounter Courses (Anglican expression): John and Sara Wheatley, 4 Hall Place Gardens, St Albans, Herts AL1 3SP.

Marriage Enrichment Courses: Ron and Rosemary Foyle, The Association for Marriage Enrichment, c/o The Westminster Pastoral Foundation, 23 Kensington Square, London W8 5HN.

Marriage Guidance Association: see local phone directory (courses in marriage counselling, by selection only). New name – RELATE.

Mission to Marriage: David and Joyce Ames, Beck House, Beck Row, Mildenhall, Bury St Edmunds, Suffolk IP28 7DP.

The North of England Christian Healing Trust: Spennithorne Hall, Leyburn, N. Yorkshire DL8 5PR.
Mainstream/Sacramental.

Personal Growth Courses in Counselling and Spirituality: Rev. B. Hawker, c/o Emmaus House, Clifton Hill, Bristol.

The Richmond Fellowship: (counselling and rehabilitation), 8 Addison Road, London W14 (071 603 6373).

Samaritans: see local phone directory. (Counselling training for telephone ministry.)

University Extra-mural Courses: Polytechnic or College courses in counselling.

Various Christian counselling agencies are now springing up in different towns, e.g.

Network, 31 College Green, Bristol BS1 5TB;

Compass, 25 Hope Street, Liverpool, Merseyside L1 9BQ;

Christian Caring, Old School, 61 St Barnabas Road, Cambridge CB1 2BX;

Post Green Pastoral Centre, 56 Dorchester Road, Lytchett Minster, Poole, Dorset BH16 6JE;

The Oxford Christian Institute for Counselling; 11 Norham Gardens, Oxford OX2 6PS.

The Pastoral Foundation, 12 Chamberlain Road, Edinburgh EH10 4DN.

WEA Courses: Workers' Educational Association often hold evening classes locally.

Westminster Pastoral Foundation: (for the training and supervision of counsellors, full-time and part-time courses) 23 Kensington Square, London W8 5HN.

Mainstream/liberal emphasis. Basis: analytical psychotherapy.

Wholeness through Christ: details from Miss Y. Cowley, c/o 2 Balmoral Crescent, Oswestry, Shropshire SY11 2XG.

An explicitly Biblical counselling model – charismatic.

GESTALT TRAINING IN THE UK

Agencies and workers listed below are not necessarily committed to the Christian beliefs of the present writer.

BRIGHTON
JACKIE CLEMENTS: private practice in Newhaven. Training programme for the medical profession and a two-year certificate course for established practitioners.
Address: 29 Meeching Road, Newhaven, Sussex.

BRISTOL AND SW
MALCOLM PARLETT: private practice and training programme, founded Bristol Gestalt Network. Trainer with Metanoia and Gestalt Centre.
Contact: Dr M. R. Parlett, 5 York Place, Clifton, Bristol BS8 1AH.

CAMBRIDGE
HELEN MCLEAN: private practice with training programme. Trainer with Gestalt Psychotherapy Institute, and Gestalt Centre, London.
Address: 5 Kimberley Road, Cambridge.

LONDON
THE GESTALT CENTRE: four-year diploma course to practitioner-level. Three-year basic training to incorporate Gestalt into other work. Low-cost therapy scheme with therapists in the Advanced Training Programme. In-service programme for experienced practitioners and trainers with international leaders at the 'growing edge' of Gestalt.
Contact: Judith Leary-Tanner, 64 Warwick Road, St Albans, Herts AL1 4DL.

METANOIA: three-year training programme (to follow a previous qualification in the helping professions), based on a series of five-day residential workshops. Diploma awarded on number of training hours completed: trainees can adjust the time-scale to suit their needs, pace and energy. Diploma awarded by the Gestalt Psychotherapy Training Institute, 13 North Common Road, London W5 2QB.

PELLIN CENTRE: one-year diploma training course for those wishing to use Gestalt in their professional work. Participants can continue with training reaching practitioner-level in four years.
Address: 43 Killyon Road, London SW8 2XS.

SPECTRUM: Four therapists run Supervision groups, private work, intensives, women's groups, residential workshops, sexuality programme, one-day and weekend workshops.
Address: 55 Dartmouth Park Road, London NW5 1SL.

LONDON, HULL, LEEDS
JANE PUDDY has private practice, works with the Gestalt Centre; runs training programmes.
Address: c/o 192 Goldhurst Terrace, London NW6.

MANCHESTER
THE MANCHESTER GESTALT CENTRE: individual and group therapy. Courses in Gestalt. Fundamentals, Training and stress-management and work for establishment groups.
Address: 270 Dickenson Road, Manchester M13 0YL.

MIDLANDS
THE ENGLISH GESTALT INSTITUTE: Four-year course to practitioner level.
Address: 67 Cubbington Road, Leamington Spa CV32 7AQ.

NOTTINGHAM
KEN EVANS, private practice; three-year training geared towards health service professionals.
Address: Brandon House, 9 Burlington Road, Sherwood, Nottingham NG5 2GR.

SCOTLAND
GESTALT TRAINING SERVICES offer ongoing training groups over three to four years for those wishing to use Gestalt in their own disciplines. Training in a residential setting of at least four weeks per year over four years.
Contact: John Whitley, 19 Primrose Bank Road, Edinburgh EH5 3JQ.